"...An agency in New Zealand took successful action against its former Managing Director and Creative Director who had walked out with 17 members of the staff and nine accounts. Gentle reader, you have been warned!"

Ogilvy on Advertising, page 62

This is the inside story of how a breakaway agency in tiny New Zealand sent the multinationals in London, New York, Paris and Sydney into shock and confusion. Meanwhile, advertising guru David Ogilvy implies they didn't get away with it! Or, did they?

PASSION WITHOUT JUSTICE®

D. Richard Truman

Editor: Professor Roy Wilson

Trafford Publishing

Canada • USA • UK • Europe

Order this book online at www.trafford.com/07-1739
or email orders@trafford.com

Most Trafford titles are also available at major online book retailers.

© Copyright 2007 D. Richard Truman.
All rights reserved. No part of this publication may be reproduced, stored in a retrieval system, or transmitted, in any form or by any means, electronic, mechanical, photocopying, recording, or otherwise, without the written prior permission of the author.

Note for Librarians: A cataloguing record for this book is available from Library and Archives Canada at www.collectionscanada.ca/amicus/index-e.html

Printed in Victoria, BC, Canada.
Editor in Chief: Professor Roy Wilson
Cover Design: Michelle K. Stafford

ISBN: 978-1-4251-4199-8

We at Trafford believe that it is the responsibility of us all, as both individuals and corporations, to make choices that are environmentally and socially sound. You, in turn, are supporting this responsible conduct each time you purchase a Trafford book, or make use of our publishing services. To find out how you are helping, please visit www.trafford.com/responsiblepublishing.html

Our mission is to efficiently provide the world's finest, most comprehensive book publishing service, enabling every author to experience success. To find out how to publish your book, your way, and have it available worldwide, visit us online at www.trafford.com/10510

 www.trafford.com

North America & international
toll-free: 1 888 232 4444 (USA & Canada)
phone: 250 383 6864 ♦ fax: 250 383 6804 ♦ email: info@trafford.com

The United Kingdom & Europe
phone: +44 (0)1865 722 113 ♦ local rate: 0845 230 9601
facsimile: +44 (0)1865 722 868 ♦ email: info.uk@trafford.com

10 9 8 7 6 5 4 3 2

*This book is dedicated to
three brave women,
who suffered the most,
but complained the least:
Beverley E. Truman
Anita Murphy &
Shirley Harris.*

Acknowledgements

There are many people to thank, so I'll keep it brief. Certainly at the top of the list are partners, co-workers, friends, suppliers and clients from the hey-day of a golden age in New Zealand. Fortunately, I've been able to converse by "e-mail" with some, including Mike Howard, David Russell, Len and Sue Birch, former neighbors and others, to verify a lot of what is contained within the narrative.

Marsha Appel of the American Association of Advertising Agencies (AAAA) in New York provided invaluable information to help compile industry facts and figures in the ebb and flow of ad agency empires.

Bruce Harris must also be thanked for supplying information from the major player on the other side of the battle - Lintas. Without the support of Harris, much information would have been lost to history or might have been misinterpreted in the heat of battle.

Finally, I must thank my family for their invaluable input and Roy Wilson, my indefatigable editor who always encourages me to write a better story than I think I'm able. And my indomitable art director, Michelle Kathleen Stafford, who battles weighty eyelids to meet demanding schedules and numerous changes inflicted by eagle-eyed editors.

I am disappointed that I have been unable to review matters with my old partner David Murphy, despite a two-year search to track him down. Murphy is an enigmatic man, much admired from a professional point of view. Others will disagree and see him quite differently. His help, too, is momentarily lost to history.

The wonderful people of New Zealand must be thanked, too, especially our closest stalwart neighbors, the Springs and their children Mark and Angela, as well as Mark and Colleen Yagusch and their offspring David, Mark and Carolyn.

MANY THANKS TO THE GOOD TALENTED PEOPLE THAT TAUGHT ME SO MUCH:

David Bailey, Therese Birch, Beth Dale, David Downham, Michael Forde, Andrea Gordon, Robin Hale, Terry Hall, Mike Howard, Maggie McKean, Linda McNab, Jon Muir, Jill Ridgewell, Tim Roberts, Dave Russell, Graham Small, Nicole Smith, Kevin Stewart, Joanne Svensen, Lindsey Wilkinson, Jane Wilmott, and Julie Yonge.

THE GUY WHO WOKE US UP IN THE MORNING:

Blackie and the mad gang at Radio Haraki and the hundreds of others who engaged us through the radio waves.

AND WHO CAN FORGET GREAT CLIENTS LIKE:

Bill Peake, Paul Brosnahan, Peter Maher, John Pilkington, and Arthur Lane from Aulsebrooks - Bob Godward and Arthur Deethe from Dominion TV Rentals - Don Gemmell, Geoff Holland, Ted Eady, David Dow and Derek Lawley from James Hardie - Richard Riley, Hugh Perrett and M. Mahaffie from Foodstuffs - Teresa Reynolds and Steven Fisher from the Spirit of New Zealand - J. Burridge, John Cameron, Alan Steedman, Alf Pollard, Revell Brownie and Jim McGillivray from Feltex - Colin Martin and Ken Holmes from Thorn - Alistair Sutherland from Spalding - Dick Brunton and Pauline Colmar from Colmar Brunton - Nigel Hamley from Smith and Nephew - Bryce Herbert and Ken Leonard from Continental Cigar - Rick Kneebone, Alan Bates from Kensington Carpets.

AND SPECIAL MOMENTARY PLAYERS LIKE:

Bob Wardlaw, Doug Graham, David Ross, David Fern, Jonathon Holloway, Ron Clout, Richard Nugent, Terry Prince and Vic Bowyer from Kingswood. Michael Thomas from Feltex Print. Wayne Williamson from Nova. Steven Watson from Parnell Printers. John Webb from VID COM. Len Burch and Sue Robinson from Carlaw Station. Bob Jackson and Bonnie Low from Mascot. Dennis Hitchcock, Rod Proud, John Woodruffe, David Waters, Norman Elder and John Blick from Interfilm. Mike Johnson and Bob Gould from Bluesky Travel. Alex Fowler from Datsun. B MacInness and Murray Clark, Mike Clarke, A Franz and J. B. Napier and the hundreds of others I failed to locate in my research efforts.

And of course the family we knew and loved most, David and Anita Murphy and their children, Matthew and Amanda.

We all agree on one thing, though -

"… as life is action and passion, it is required of a man that he should share the passion and action of his time at peril of being judged not to have lived."
                                                       Oliver Wendell Holmes Jr. 1884

Contents

Acknowledgments	5
Prologue	13
Understanding the Ad Biz	17
The Key Players	21

Chapter 1
The Walkout is a Better Beginning 27
    Everyone out – away they went 27
    Why did it happen? 32

Chapter 2
265 Halcyon Days Earlier 35
    Victoria Avenue – memories of an old Queen 39
    Getting "down-under," to work 42
    New faces jump on board 43
    Little blue people walk into my pocket 46

Chapter 3
The Rewards of Smart 49
    Carpets from the "wood of the ship" 50
    A taste of home 52
    Know the market 54

Chapter 4
Sydney and Kenny 61
    Losing without ever losing 65
    Moving with the times 69

Chapter 5
No, Nobody's Listening 73
    The squeal of tireds 73
    A move to Rama Rama 75
    Drinking, womanizing and playing around 76
    "Just like that!" 79
    "She'll be right mate" 81

Chapter 6
Coming Together — 85
- Giving birth at Boodles — 89
- I have an idea — 91
- A fateful decision — 92

Chapter 7
A Final Stupid Act — 95
- To party – without reason — 95
- A hint from "Tusitala" — 97
- A wake-up call — 98
- The spy museum of the South Pacific — 99
- Illusions are illusory — 102
- You've got ten minutes, go! — 103
- Upon reflection! — 104

Chapter 8
Hey, We Just Quit! — 105

Chapter 9
Back 265 Days to Chapter 1 — 109

Chapter 10
A New Era Dawns. A Battle Begins — 111
- David vs. Goliath — 111
- Goliath is slow off the mark — 113
- A disappointing start for Lintas — 116
- The first stone is lobbed and it hurt — 117
- Lintas throws more deadly blows — 118
- A crushing blow hits the mark — 118
- The one that hurt the most — 120
- Our mole is "flicked" — 121

Chapter 11
Lintas Has Momentum & Taunts Us — 123
- Lintas hit the funny bone — 124
- Murphy Truman is defiant — 126
- A Royal interruption — 128
- The "saga" changes course — 131
- Thorn EMI tunes in — 132

CHAPTER 12
AN ANGEL OF MERCY — **135**
    CHRISTMAS WITH THE LIGHTS OFF — 137

CHAPTER 13
ALL TOGETHER AGAIN — **141**
    IT'S OFF TO WORK WE GO — 141
    LINTAS' WIGGLING CONTINUES — 143
    CRACKERS, WOOL AND FLYING HIGH! — 145
    OFF TO THE STONEMASON'S — 150
    SHOOTING IN THE WHEAT FIELDS — 152
    FINDING DINOSAURS — 154

CHAPTER 14
"DOWNHAM, I JUST CANT DO IT" — **159**
    GLOBE HOPPING TO TROUBLE — 160
    CANNES AND CAN'TS — 161
    NGAPUI GONE – VICTORIA'S BACK — 165
    "LINTAS WALKOUT: HAVE THEY GOT AWAY WITH IT?" — 168

CHAPTER 15
THE LAST LAUGH — **171**
    THREE LITTLE PRIGS - MARION, DAVID AND BRIAN — 172
    AIR ON A SHOE STRING — 175
    JERUSALEM COCK-UP — 178
    TO THE LAND OF TURNER — 181

CHAPTER 16
HOME IS WHERE THE HOUSE IS — **185**
    ONE YEAR AFTER THE FACT — 186
    SNOW IS NOT A FOUR-LETTER WORD — 188
    THE END IS NEAR — 188

CHAPTER 17
BAILING OUT – SELLING UP — **193**
    IT FINALLY HIT — 193
    WESTPAC TOWERS AHEAD — 196
    A BEAUTIFUL PRINCESS COMES CALLING — 198
    ANITA'S GIFT — 199
    MURPHY TRUMAN GOES INTERNATIONAL — 201

Chapter 18
We're Going, We're Gone — 203

Chapter 19
Losers & Winners — 205
    The losers? — 205
    The winners? — 208

Chapter 20
In Summary — 211
A Special Tribute — 213

About the Author — 215
About the Editor — 217

PROLOGUE

The worldwide advertising industry is big and dazzling, with the might of a great military machine, but with the steadiness of Jell-O. It hangs together, just!

More than $427 billion (U.S. dollars) is spent annually to encourage the public to buy things, making advertising one of mankind's largest and most influential industries, according to a report by Publicis Group Zenith Optimedia 2006.

Canadian Business, in September 2006 reported the industry attracts top career-hunters, with 12.9% of university graduates wanting to work in glamorous, high paying advertising and marketing positions. And it's an industry that puffs up talent, pays well, and shuffles people around the globe with complete ease.

Advertising shapes how people think, tricking the masses into responding and acting in a predetermined way. The messages agencies communicate make consumers buy products and feel good, and in most societies will determine the choice of governments and leaders who'll rule the world.

Canadian humorist Stephen Butler Leacock summed it up nicely when he said, "Advertising may be described as the science of arresting the human intelligence long enough to get money from it."

On the positive side, industry players influence the prices you pay for a product or service, and it's usually low, because of the fierce competition and rivalry that is generated. The contribution to wealth generation by industry leaders is significant, too, and that's probably a good thing.

The bad side is, consumers pay for things they don't really need and chuck out things before their sell-by date, creating vast waste and garbage.

So it's good and it's bad.

This book looks inside the industry at a few of the people and companies that are best at playing the game - the professionals, both big and small.

In the eighties, when this story takes place, one of the giants is a company called SSC&B Lintas, a unit of the Interpublic Group of Cos. Its roots go back to 1879, when it began as the in-house advertising agency for Lever Brothers (Unilever). For the sake of brevity, we'll call it Lintas. In 1981, its worldwide billings were $1,168,319,000, of which the greater chunk, $890,512,000 (75%), came from outside the U.S.A. Small offices in New Zealand and other out-of-the-way foreign offices contribute handsomely to its profitability.

This is the story of an incident in a small Lintas office in New Zealand that shouldn't have happened. Certainly not the way it is reported. The managing director and the creative director resign to set up on their own agency. Soon, most of the staff and all of the clients follow them to their new agency, never to return to Lintas. This is true. Revenge is in the air.

The incident provokes the billion-dollar leviathan, prodding the sleeping giant into a form of revenge - on an unprecedented scale. The big guy decides to "crush" the little guy for what it calls legal misbehavior. Goliath is determined to squash David Murphy, the managing director, and Richard Truman, the creative director and author of this story.

What leads to the "walkout?" Who wins the legal battle and who loses the war?

Some recollections will be disputed, but I've made a valiant effort to be fair and report facts as I recall them. In most instances, I've relied on court documents, legal correspondence and media reports to verify evidence reported here.

I have not had the privilege of working with my ex-partner David Murphy to validate his point of view. But I was there and shared most of the same experiences. Murphy is impossible to track down, despite placing ads in local newspapers, letters to the editor, correspondence, both written and e-mailed to familiar names in Auckland and to a lost network of friends and associates.

An old nemesis, Bruce Harris, long retired from Lintas, suddenly reappeared. Harris represented Lintas in the court battle long ago. He has been very helpful in keeping my enthusiasm for the breakaway in check. Opinions may differ, but we still hold firmly to our beliefs.

A few lines in a book by the late David Ogilvy, a giant in the industry, are the reason I pursued the matter - to disprove Ogilvy's conclusion. The hammer of extreme law, after all, does produce extreme distress.

For some players, it is an ordeal best forgotten. I want justice, even if it's for the sake of reputations and a passion for fairness.

For the wives, it was a hardship. The incident was hidden from the view of my children, but the setting of New Zealand is remembered fondly.

"Passion Without Justice" is a story that might encourage some to be passionate about their beliefs, while most might hesitate.

This powerful industry must set titanium-clad rules of conduct if it is to escape from the Jell-O mould in the future.

Understanding the Ad Biz

Before you read on, I will attempt to explain what an ad agency is, in simple terms.

The ad agency is independent from clients or customers. Agencies are hired by companies like Coke, General Motors or Nabisco to provide independent advice to their marketing honchos scattered around the free-trading globe.

It's essential that ad agencies provide an independent point of view for clients, as opposed to them hiring internal staff to handle marketing chores. It's just too expensive and inside staff often become set in their ways and sheltered from reality. The beauty is, if the ad agency doesn't get the sales results a company like Coke is seeking, the contract is terminated and the agency replaced by others always chasing companies to win their business.

Ad agencies create, expand and maintain customers for clients by explaining to consumers why these companies offer the best product or service at the best price. Good marketing people at good ad agencies take bold actions to define, create, grow, develop, maintain, defend and own markets for their clients.

Industry gurus like Al Ries and Jack Trout define marketing as a "war" between competitors. Therefore, you need the best generals. Terms like attack, frontal assault, pincer movement and guerilla warfare are bandied about with ease. "In strategy it is important to see distant things as if they are close and to take a distanced view of close things," and "Suppress the enemy's useful actions but allow his useless actions" are phrases derived from a 17th century classic text: Miyamoto Musashi's A BOOK OF FIVE RINGS. So after five centuries, ad agencies are still engaged in an ongoing war with the competition, filled with strategies reminiscent of war games.

While hardly academic, the four Ps of marketing - product, pricing, promotion and placement - are still in practice. Product is easy to understand: create a product that is needed and will be purchased. Pricing, too, is tricky, but obvious. Promotion is really advertising, sales promotion, public relations (PR) and refers to the many ways we promote the product, brand or company. Placement is, simply, distribution. Getting the product to the right store and placing it on the right shelf, from top to bottom, or into the right bin, on aisle two.

This is the marketing mix that agencies are battling to control, partially or completely. Methods include conducting research to delve into the customers' minds to determine the exact product they want us to produce.

The advice the Lintas agency provides to clients in Auckland ranges over a number of categories, from creating ads and displays in stores, to television and radio commercials meant to drive shoppers to the correct store.

Lintas Auckland also provides media advice, telling clients which media is most effective in reaching their customers. Then, agencies buy "space" for client firms, in the agreed media. It's a major source of revenue, as they provide a commission payable to agencies. It can be as high as 20% of the cost of the purchase.

Research and planning is also provided by the New Zealand office, as well as other obscure or new wave tricks that help the agency's clients to sell their products or provide a more profitable and better service.

Yes, in tiny New Zealand, the agency provides total marketing services, branding strategies and sales promotion. All big and profitable stuff for agencies; all handled by the experienced, highly educated staff that big agencies bring to the table from offices around the world. They're not cheap, by any means; they're expensive people, often hard to attract and even more difficult to keep.

Managing directors, CEOs or presidents do the predictable tasks and run the operations. They usually report to regional people around the globe who in turn salute the bosses in the big centers of marketing in London, Paris or New York.

Account service people are the sinews that bind client needs and agency offerings; they bridge the gap. They listen to client needs, involve agency specialists in a plan, and then deliver solutions to clients' complex problems. It's a tough no-nonsense business activity only survived by the talented and the determined.

Creative people write the ads, or create the look of the advertising that is designed to force consumers to listen to a storyline while being seduced by the message. The leaders are creative directors, supported by writers, art directors, typographers and producers who put the television and radio commercials together. They are rarely failed artists, but are extraordinarily talented and well-trained opinion benders who know how to win a customer over. The top creative minds are usually paid far more than the managers and the account services stokers. The top ones who create great "ideas" and win awards are wooed away by competitors with big money. Not a pleasant profession, but it can give you highs that cannot be delivered in any other profession.

Research gurus and planners are the ones who solve the complex riddles and devise strategic plans that are meant to trap or trick customers into buying. The best are some of the brightest and highest paid minds in the business world today.

Greasing the wheels are the production people who put things together, along with the specialists who create stunning display material and write skilled direct marketing programs that normally come in the mail and try to convince you to join this bank, change credit cards or join an organization. It is now such an art and science that agencies know how many breaths you take each day opening the mail.

Ad agencies around the world range from one-man-band operations in a garage, to the infamous WPP Group of Britain, valued at $48 billion dollars, or Publicis of France, at $35 billion, or the American Interpublic Group, at nearly $28 billion. History tells us the big guys are growing rapidly by gobbling up the little guys in their garages along the way. It is no different than other industries: size is muscle and shock and awe win wars.

This enormous advertising and marketing industry is presently spending around half a trillion dollars a year worldwide and growing faster than most. Look out Exxon Mobil, Wal-Mart and Royal Dutch Shell. The few big ad agency groups left are on the march to world domination. The reason for growth is easy to understand. Ad agencies are needed to keep the wheels of commerce humming and profits pouring into the pockets of shareholders, in a savagely competitive global shoot-out for supremacy. Agencies are in demand.

This is the tale of one of the world giants and its battle with a smaller office that wants to be listened to but ultimately is forced to operate differently. It's a bloody battle with worldwide noise, leading to joy and celebration, humility and ruin, along with unexpected death and the finality of suicide.

The Key Players

There are many, but three should be singled out and understood from the beginning.

David J. Murphy is central to the story. Without Murphy, there is no tale to tell. He provokes the giant-agency world and initiates change that will impact many lives for years to come.

Murphy, or Murf, as he's called by friends, was born in London, England. He joined the Northern Rhodesia police force, and worked on the Belgian Congo border for three years, finally working in a copper mine. Murf knew that you had to have iron in the blood to survive. In 1964, he emigrated to the sun, intending to join the New Zealand navy, but balked and decided to settle in New Zealand.

David J. Murphy

Today he's a young forty, with fire in the belly and the energy of a typhoon. Murphy is passion personified, both good and questionable. If he likes something, he runs with it. If he doesn't, he provokes change. The London lad is a good looking man, tall like an English bobby, with jet black hair and a heavy moustache that smiles before his lips. Erect as a viola and when debating a point is able to fiddle with the best. Murphy has a jaunty air, is attractive to women and is charismatic – he's a natural salesman without realizing it and at times can be blown along by his own wind.

In September of 1971, he began his career in the advertising business at Woolworths, and is soon on the bridge at SSC&B Lintas in Wellington.

As a scrapper in a somewhat lifeless market, he shows early promise as new accounts are added to the roster. A second Lintas office is opened in 1973 on Cheshire Street in the bustling city of Auckland. The largest city in New Zealand is quickly becoming the center of commerce in the country. New head offices are springing up like dandelions and that's where he wants to be.

Three years later, December 14, 1976, he's appointed a director of the company. His appointment is never laid to paper: he works contract-free. An error by Lintas, later regretted.

Two years later, on July 3, 1978, further praise is heaped on the grinning Murphy when he's appointed managing director for the whole of New Zealand. The spring in his step propels him to top dog in a country he adores.

By now, Murphy is married to a wonderful New Zealand beauty, Anita, and they soon have a family, son Matthew and daughter Amanda. Two wonderful children fill their home with the sounds of love and laughter.

The same year, Murphy moves to Auckland and transfers the head office from Wellington to Auckland, because that's where decisions are being made. The Auckland office quickly feels the rush of growth under his stewardship and he's spotted as an up-and-comer at world conferences.

By 1982, he is more fully involved with client business. Being managing director has its weaknesses, he will say. It isn't where the action is. He also realizes his strengths as a marketing person, and his conceptual thinking begins to bear fruit in an extraordinary way. Murphy is on his way as a marketing strategist and is blazing a trail.

His triumph is attributed to a belief, *"The client wants to be proud of its agency, the people there and the product they put out, so I have always tried to project an image of energy, enthusiasm and excitement and have always looked for it in the people I have employed."*

This is all I recall about Murphy from memory and scraps of paper he left behind.

He now asks Lintas for help in adding global strength to his team, to prepare them for dominance in the New Zealand market. Murphy travels the world looking for professional help and finds Richard Truman in Toronto, Canada.

The other lead character is the author, **D. Richard Truman**, an adman from humble origins in Hamilton,

D. Richard Truman

Canada, who ends up on the international stage as a global creative director.

I learned about the advertising and communications business in Art College. But I started quite accidentally as a "visualizer;" the person charged with doing a "layout" that looks like the final ad when it appears. It's amazing what can be done to trick the eye with a pencil, brush and a few magic-markers. Unfortunately, this profession met its death in the twenty-first century.

I soon realize it's not too difficult to become an art director. The boss man who takes charge of the look of ads or of a television commercial is the art director. Glamorous title, but not too difficult to manage, as long as you have an ability to sell what you've created to a client. Fortunately, I've inherited my mother's loose lips and manage to convince most listeners that I know what I'm talking about.

After life as an art director, I discover you make a better living if you write the words for an ad as well: silly things like headlines and "slogans," a term I dislike. So that is the next hurdle to leap over.

By 1964, I am attracted to swinging London by the Beatles and their life-altering demand for world change and the dismantling of class order and privilege. I return to college and study at the BBC to learn about making television commercials and the psychology of communications. It is perhaps the best move ever, as the British know how to create powerful "soft" advertising and the learning curve shot straight up. Humour, the double entendre: the power of sex, puppies and babies; the British craftsmen are still masters of soft advertising, because it works.

After joining a multinational agency group, I was transferred from London to Africa, to Paris, then Brussels and finally back to Canada. In the meantime, I had become a creative director and was responsible for creating global campaigns for clients from Wrigley's and General Mills to Chrysler, Ford, Burger King, Unilever and General Motors, with dozens of big league brands under my belt in between. Awards and industry fame follow. My ticket to international success is assured. I am in demand.

I marry a delightful British girl and have two children, Michelle and Nicole, both in their single digits when they arrive in New Zealand.

One of the great frustrations for Canadians in the ad business is the inability to practice the advertising craft, because so much material is created in the USA and simply sent to Canada. My first job at MacLaren Advertising in Toronto was to paint over American flags with Canadian flags, for General Motors' ads originally created and photographed in the USA. It drove me out of Canada once and is about to do it again as this story begins.

That's when a friend from Lintas telephones and suggests a lunch with the managing director of the New Zealand office of Lintas. I am to meet with a David Murphy from Lintas, an agency group I'd worked with before and like. Add the thought of warmth and sunshine in the middle of winter and creative freedom. Then take away the four-letter word "snow," and the rest is history.

The final leviathan to be introduced is **Bruce Harris**, the CEO Chairman of Lintas, in Sydney, Australia.

Harris is an Australian, born in the west coast city of Perth. He relocated to Sydney, because that's where the action was at the time.

Upstart Harris joined Lintas in mid-1946, then moved to George Patterson, another giant advertising agency in Sydney. Harris was an account director at Patterson for three years. A headhunter convinced him to leave Patterson to rejoin Lintas as Creative Director. He swiftly shot up the ranks from writer to CEO over his thirty-five year career. Harris, like me, began his career as a creative person.

Bruce Harris

He travelled the world as an Australian ambassador for Lintas, and quickly found favour with European and American leaders. Harris had the necessary veneer and was listened to.

By 1981, he's about to complete his final year at Lintas before saying goodbye to an industry he loves, to move on to something different. This is to be his last year in the business. At age 57 he is going to slow down, in a business that will not let you slow down.

His replacement, Brit Roger Neill, settles in Australia in March of 1981 and is being readied to take the big chair from Harris in January 1982.

Harris's wife Shirley and three daughters, Jennifer, Vicki and Merrilee, welcome the prospect of seeing more of "dad." Other interests, from managing part of his brother's business, to writing and publishing, keep him active. He's the kind of person who dislikes being inactive; he likes to be referred to as a really busy guy.

His brother Rolf is a celebrity in the UK and Australia and Bruce will remain involved in helping his brother's long career as singer, entertainer, cartoonist, artist and overall creative guy with concerts and TV shows that leap around the world.

With three months to go before stepping down, a phone call from across the Tasman will change his careful sequestration, as he's called upon to sort out a mess.

Let the story begin.

Chapter 1

THE WALKOUT IS A BETTER BEGINNING

EVERYONE OUT - AWAY THEY WENT

100 Greys Avenue
Auckland, New Zealand
Sept 22, 1981, Tuesday, 4:00 P.M.
The Boardroom

The staff is notified an announcement will be made in the boardroom.

September is late winter in New Zealand. The day is overcast and lifeless; colour is drained from everything in view. A foreboding fills the air, signaling trouble ahead. Staff trundle along darkened hallways, suspicious of what they're heading toward.

A few know what is going to happen. Some are apprehensive; many have started rumours distant from the truth. Only managing director David Murphy, Richard Truman, and five senior staff are aware of what is about to happen.

As part of a plan, insiders ask our "mole" to stay away that day, to remain in the dark about events that will soon unfold, as we need him to report the resignations to the regional office in Sydney, after the announcement. This way, they will rely on his loyalty in the hours ahead, believing he is devoted to Lintas. So the mole isn't going to resign that day; it's part of a plan. He stays with the firm, along with twenty or so staff, during the turbulent days ahead, reporting their moves back to us, often on an hourly basis, to keep us abreast of their maneuvers.

The mood is somber; the look on faces is gothic.

The room is filled to the gunnels with agency staff, with the exception of our mole. Most stand or lean against walls, as a memo issued earlier said a major announcement is to be made at four in the afternoon.

New Zealand SSC&B Lintas managing director David Murphy stands up to speak. The tall, good-looking Murphy, with the "Chewbacca" moustache, is one of New Zealand's best strategic minds. In a larger market with muscle and voice, this forty-two year old, with presence and charisma, would have bounded to the top in record time. He is razor-sharp; his personality is pressed like Sunday trousers. But being in tiny New Zealand left him a little transparent to the string-pullers at head offices in London, Paris, New York and Sydney. Even though small offices kick buckets of green, up to 75% of the revenue, into the coffers of the multinationals, this one is overlooked.

At precisely 4:00 P.M. David walks to the side of the room and stands near the fireplace. He looks around anxiously, clears his throat and begins to make this historic announcement. Although he's prepared notes, he seems to ignore them and speaks from the heart. It's deathly quiet with the exception of an annoying winter fly.

He indicates to the gathering that he has been thinking about the matter he's about to raise for a long time and that he has decided to *tender his resignation* to be effective at 5:00 P.M. today. He also says he will try to operate an advertising agency on his own, as evidenced later, under oath, by Cherie Susanne Ryan. A hush silences the room, except for the rustle of feet and the crack of neck-muscles looking for friends among the shocked faces.

I'm next on my feet, shuffling uneasily, to explain why I will also be leaving. Tim Roberts is next, followed by other key staff who join the string of resignations from the office that afternoon. Most truly unexpected.

Tears flow; bodies caress one another. Sadness and confusion stir the air. Someone shouts, "If you're going, so am I," as they voluntarily sign letters of resignation addressed to David Downham, the company commercial manager.

All to be telexed to Australian head office in Sydney by 5:00 P.M., or within minutes of the resignations on the 22nd.

Tim's resignation is followed by Therese, Lindsey, Beth, Robin, Kevin, Andrea, Jon, Linda, Mike, Nicole, Julie, Michael, Jillian, Joanne, David and another David. That's seventeen along with David and me: a total of nineteen bodies. The fourth David, David Downham, the commercial manager, will be the one to send the resignations to the regional head office in Sydney, Australia. Wednesday, September 23 at 10 A.M., Downham telephones Michael O'Sullivan, a Lintas director in Wellington, to say that he's received a resignation from Mr. Murphy and that he is going to telephone Bruce Harris, the area co-coordinator of the group. The resignation notice does not reach Sydney until Friday, September 25, three days later.

Following our announcement on September 22, a stunned body of unemployed Lintas employees burst into the grey light of a winter evening, shaken by events. What had they done?

The actions this day will be reported repeatedly in the months ahead. The local rags and the international press, along with pundits and lawyers who will grow fat on both sides of the argument, soon gravitate toward the headlines.

The biggest storm-out in New Zealand advertising history has begun: perhaps the biggest walkout in Australasian advertising history and one of the most striking putsches in the world of advertising dominated by the fat multinationals.

What made this particularly galling is that the SSC&B Lintas agency is 51% owned by Unilever, the world's biggest food products producer, with global sales of $6.57 billion, according to the *New York Times* archives *(earnings up at Unilever Group, May 19, 1981)* and 49% by Interpublic of New York, the world's largest advertising and marketing group at the time.

New York, London, Paris and Sydney, Australia must now be summoned into action.

This is a disaster with international ramifications. The headlights are on and the horn is bleating. But, it could have been prevented!

The local rags grabbed hold of the news first and pounded out headlines. Soon, news spread around the world as head offices in Paris, London and New York try to locate New Zealand on a map.

Fingers ultimately find it and the spotlight is shone on tiny New Zealand, for all the wrong reasons.

Don Farmer, a reporter with the *Sunday News*, probably nailed it first and best. The local rags are all looking for an angle.

Ad staff get up and go, is the bold headline pumped out by the *Sunday News*. His report states, *"The trendy world of advertising has been thrown into turmoil with the Auckland staff of a leading agency staging what is believed to be the biggest walkout in New Zealand's advertising history.*

Twenty-four employees of the world-renowned SSC&B Lintas agency have left and set up a rival firm.

They include the managing director and creative director.

Only commercial manager David Downham and two girls remain in the Auckland office.

Heading the shock exodus was former managing director David Murphy. He told Sunday News this week he decided to resign after "battling with Lintas all year over a number of issues - These included my salary and my personal career and I resigned when I realized Lintas couldn't offer me a future."

"Once I had made up my mind to quit I told the staff and most of them decided to come with me…I didn't try to spirit them away," Mr. Murphy said.

Creative director Richard Truman joined the rebel entourage and the group spent this week setting up the Murphy Truman advertising agency on Anzac Avenue.

The shock walkout resulted in the lightning arrival in New Zealand of Mr. Bruce Harris, chairman of the company's Australian operations (at 157 Walker Street, in North Sydney.) Mr. Harris is brother of entertainer Rolf Harris.

He told Sunday News that Mr. Murphy, as a director and "responsible officer," had resigned and left the firm on the same day.

"That breaks the rules of decent business practice and could be seen as an irresponsible thing to do."

"It's true a number of staff members left with him...but I don't believe our Auckland agency is wiped out," said Mr. Harris.

He said his visit (Monday, September 28 – 6 days after the walk-out) to New Zealand was for the express purpose of getting the Auckland office back together. (But there is nothing left to put back together.)

Mr. Harris refused to comment on allegations that the new advertising agency had not only taken away staff from Lintas, but a large number of accounts too.

It is understood SSC&B Lintas recently won several major new clients.

The National Business Review ran the story the day Harris arrives, on September 28.

"In a lightning putsch last Tuesday night, Lintas's New Zealand managing director, David Murphy, telexed his unexpected resignation and walked out with 24 of the 27 staff to set up Murphy Truman Advertising."

"SSC&B Lintas's Auckland office, an arm of the world's biggest advertising empire, closed its doors last Wednesday when the New Zealand managing director walked out with most of the staff and the firm's clients to start their own advertising agency. And he reported the usual embarassment, SSC&B Lintas 51% owned by Unilever and 49% by Interpublic, is part of the Interpublic Group of New York. Interpublic is the world's largest advertising group."

"Everyone out...away they went." Warren Barrymen and others cover the story from somnambulant city, as it quickly leaks from Auckland to the international press.

Barrymen added a little more after talking with Murphy, "...I got tired of working with a rather anonymous international conglomerate and thought at this time in my career it was time to strike out on my own.

I told Truman about my plans and he decided to join me. When other staffers were told they said, 'If you two are going, so are we.' It was an amazing session Tuesday night."

Murphy said he was applying for full media accreditation and negotiating with a big multinational agency to buy up to 24.9% of his new company's shares and form an international connection.

Asked about the ethical implications of walking out with his former employer's clients, Murphy said, "If clients want to switch agencies, that's the clients' business. These guys (Lintas clients) appointed our agency yesterday." (Wednesday, September 23)

Murphy described his staff morale as "incredible."

"They wanted to be involved in something more personal than Lintas," he said.

Bruce Harris illustrated by his celebrated brother Rolf Harris

Three people scattered around the world will now be dragged into the fray: Bruce Harris, the chairman and CEO of Lintas in Sydney, Australia; Tim Green the chairman of the company at Lintas International HQ in London, England and Jean-Francois Lacour, the roving executive-director David Murphy reports to in Paris, who is in India when the flam struck.

Until these three aging stars agree on a plan and approve next moves, nothing will happen.

A few resignations have signaled a possible war on an unprecedented level.

In an upcoming and extraordinary court case, the first in British legal history, a victory for Lintas will resolve whether Murphy and Truman broke fiduciary trust. The break-out is going global, and it will cost money.

The world's billion dollar empires are about to attempt to crush David and me for quitting. Will Goliath succeed in this precedent-setting conflict?

Why did it happen?

In a small, pleasant country like New Zealand, it's the kind of big news Kiwis don't want to read about because it's embarrassing: the biggest shock in the history of the advertising industry. No, it's not original, it has happened before. But this one is BIG news: it's the biggest.

As reported, an entire company bolts from its foreign owners, a giant multinational, and takes all of the big advertising accounts and employees with it and appears to get away with it. That hurts.

While SSC&B in London, Paris, New York, and Sydney is not watching, the walkout half a globe away, is over within minutes.

London, at the time, is the centre of operations for the giant Lintas network, Europe's biggest. The Paris office is another powerhouse nestled on the Seine and headed by aging and charismatic Frenchman Philipe Charmet. The gregarious and garrulous Charmet ran the kingdom like a personal fiefdom, of which he is the Patron.

As Charmet is nearing retirement age, his successor might be tipped as Jean-Francois Lacour. The hard-working and talented Lacour is a busy man with Australia, New Zealand, Asia-Pacific,

India and Greece all within his area of operations. Therefore, his discussions with Murphy in Auckland fell a few rungs on his ladder of importance. In fact, they fell off the ladder as matters in New Zealand heated up.

David Ogilvy, the guru of smarts in the advertising world globbed onto the news, or the judgement, much later and wrote on page 62-63 of *Ogilvy on Advertising* his version of the outcome this way, "*...an agency in New Zealand took successful action against its former Managing Director and Creative Director who had walked out with 17 members of the staff and nine accounts. Gentle reader, you have been warned.*"

There are many theories about what happened, but why did it happen?

A misjudgement: a couple of guys "innocently" resign to set up their own agency. Then everything falls like dominos, with everyone jumping on board, because the leaders are able and charismatic. That's one explanation.

We knew as we resigned Lintas would throw us out the same day; that's the way some multinationals acted at the time. So we left immediately.

Another theory is that it is a wonderfully orchestrated conspiracy by an egotistical madman, as a court writ would report, who will take all of the staff and accounts to set up on their own, while the owners in Paris, London and New York are blinded by distance.

The few calling it a "consensual reaction," are not paid attention to and dismissed. A consensual reaction is a euphoric emotional ground swell: everything fell into place and the staff and clients just follow the lead taken by Murphy and Truman.

But, the *real* story is much deeper, and is David Ogilvy wrong about his conclusion?

What rattled the billion dollar empires in London, Paris, New York and Sydney so much that it resulted in a state of open warfare? The world will now invade New Zealand and rip it open for inspection.

To understand *what* happened and *why* it happened let's look back 265 days, when the second half of the cocktail was arriving.

Chapter 2

265 HALCYON DAYS EARLIER

January 14, 1981
9:15 A.M.

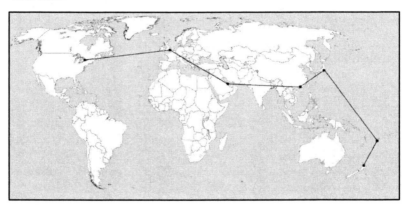

We're finally grounded after a journey that blew us from Toronto to London, to say goodbye to Beverley's family, then on to Bahrain. From the expanse of the oil kingdoms we head to Hong Kong, then onward to Tokyo.

Finally, we head south and land in Fiji for a rest at "The Fijian" on Yanuca Island, where we perfect the word "bula," a local greeting that seems to mean hello, how are you, and goodbye.

Swimming in blue lagoons, sailing and hanging out at the Black Marlin is heaven on earth for a family escaping the blast of a northern Canadian chill.

Then, after tossing off the winter blues, we're blown by a South

Pacific typhoon straight to this idyllic land of mystery. It's day one in New Zealand. I'd been here once before, while working on the Air New Zealand advertising account in London and my memories of an enchanting land remain. There's a tick approaching New Zealand that's serene and magnificently beautiful.

It's morning; a jasmine sky is streaked like the petals of an orchid. The craft banks gently east, roars over and around the aqua playground for Auckland yachties. A thousand and one white sails dot the green seas, below. The tiny 737 glides over a quilted pattern of dewy greens, spotted with fluffy white buttons that probably say "bah" if you push them. Air New Zealand purrs and descends slowly over orderly white homes, and parks its empty belly on a strip of tarmac surrounded by forty-five million sheep.

When you step outside, you breathe the sweet scent of frangipani. That's what I remember most: the air is sweet and fragrant.

My wife Beverley and two little daughters have decided it's the last time we'll shovel snow and battle the winter flu bugs that sapped our energies. This is the result.

Our home outside Toronto has been rented to Big Tom Rivers, a disc jockey with CHUM Radio. Big Tom, a 6 foot 6 inch giant of a man, is one of the greatest crazies of the era. His salary at CHUM is about the same as I'm to earn. At least we know our house will be safe until we return in three years, a little healthier and perhaps a little better off. If we like the place, the idea of staying appeals, too. Little do we know we're walking into a turbulent chapter in our lives with life-altering consequences.

But how did I end up in this particular situation? Let's look further back for a minute.

In the advertising industry, people are transferred all over the place and usually enjoy the big bucks, security and cultural bathing associated with transfers. The other fact that's comforting is that I've worked with SSC&B Lintas before, with Jules Heyndals in Brussels and Bob MacLaren, the worldwide creative director, in London. The move will be easy, as I've a high regard for the organization.

This move, however, came out of the blue, as a friend from Lintas called. I'd responded to his request and agreed to meet David Murphy, the managing director of Lintas New Zealand while he is in

Toronto. At the time, I'm a creative director with Ronalds Reynolds and am having fun with my boss, the amiable kingmaker Hank Karpus.

So it all starts as an excuse to have breakfast with an interesting guy from far away New Zealand, one of my favourite places in the world, and a chance to get back to creating original advertising, unlike picking up American advertising and changing an end title, a process that began to provoke me at Ronald Reynolds. General Mills and Texaco were both guilty of forcing Canadians to watch American television commercials produced by American agencies. It upset me greatly, as I believe advertising is cultural and should be created by Canadians and reflect our values if shown in Canada.

The breakfast with Murphy is wrapped in great fanfare and suddenly I realize this is a serious opportunity to work in the South Pacific for a few years and to create 100% original New Zealand advertising.

After breakfast at the Plaza Two, we knew we liked each other and, shock of shocks, I accept that this opportunity might work for both of us.

Within a year, Murphy wrote a promotional piece about the breakfast and said, *"In November 1980, I spent 12 hours in Toronto, Canada. The temperature was ten below. The wind blew straight down the world's longest street, Yonge Street, 1,200 miles from the Arctic. But over breakfast at the Plaza Two on Bloor Street I met a very special person who made the weather outside and the long flight from Auckland well worthwhile.*

For five years I had been fighting to build New Zealand's greatest agency, but had been frustrated by the lack of a world-class creative director. When I met Richard Truman over coffee and croissants I knew that my search was over. Richard impressed me with his ability to create, to originate. He was fluent, intelligent and concerned about the whole process of advertising. He had the experience and the personality to do the job. He joined me in Auckland three months later."

That sort of summed up where his head is at that moment, but I didn't know it at the time.

David's mission is hard-focused: to build the best agency in Australasia.

I am attracted by a couple of things: primarily, the fact that advertising produced in New Zealand has to be made in New Zealand. The Kiwi industry, like the Aussie industry, protects and develops local talent. They *can't use imported American or British advertising*. They create their own: it's the law. A Coke jingle, for example, has to be re-recorded with New Zealand singers before it can be played on their airwaves. This does incredible things for local talent and cultural industries, and years later will produce a dynamic and powerful film, television, pop music and cultural pool of talent.

Riding on the back of this policy, tiny New Zealand developed a number of great actors, directors, writers, producers, cinematographers and music people. Actors like Russell Crowe and Sam Neill will emerge. It will lead to New Zealand developing a world-quality film industry, creating great films like Peter Jackson's *"Lord of the Rings"* trilogy as well as *"King Kong"* and great epics like *"The Piano," "The Last Samurai"* and *"Race for the Zankee Zephyr,"* to name a few. I found that opportunity to be the most exhilarating of all.

The other reason is the climate, as the weather in Auckland is temperate to sub-tropical all-year-round. What's not to like?

And I like the man. He is charismatic and gushes passionately about fulfilling dreams. Murphy talks about his wife Anita and their two children, Matthew and Amanda, a little older than ours but close enough to bring them together. The man has a charm and presence that'll splice my rather wayward and unpredictable creative bursts to a world of business logic and reason. He is cool, reasoned and intellectually passionate. It's a rare opportunity that two people find each other and might be more productive together than apart.

In the business, I'm called Richard and known to be enthusiastic, infectious and believe in everything I am doing. I dropped my first name Donald years back, because it reminds me of a ribbing I took at school because of a famous duck.

So David and I suddenly realize we can be a team with sales energy and creative passion. We look to be inseparable, with chemistry similar to what I shared with CEO Brian Cronan, in London, for most of a decade. The magic has never again been duplicated, until this moment.

Accepting this challenge is a difficult decision, as I'm enjoying a string of successes with interesting advertising accounts like Canada Savings Bonds, Air Canada, General Mills and Miles Laboratories. There is no professional reason to leave, but the images David paints about New Zealand and the dream of bringing up two young daughters in a gentle land under a long white cloud excites us: sailing in the harbour, an outdoor life practically the whole year round and living in a Victorian home with a large pool, surrounded by lemon and orange groves. The ideas of shucking fresh oysters from the shoreline of nearby volcanoes and quaffing South Pacific oxygen are exhilarating thoughts, but still only a fantasy.

But doing 100% original advertising as I'd been doing in London, England for years is the kicker that excites me again.

But, is it a dream?

Within forty-eight hours, the telephone rings. David is calling from London, asking if I will join him in Auckland in one month. SSC&B Lintas agrees to a three-year transfer and will foot the travel bill to and from New Zealand, along with shipping our furnishings, and has thrown in business class travel for the family, both ways.

A glance out the window at the blue-ice forming on our front street-light and the sound of wind buffeting the trees behind our home in West Hill made the decision easy.

Victoria Avenue – Memories of an Old Queen

Within hours of our arrival, Lintas help us find a rental home in the up-market community of Remuera. A car is promised within a few days. Pick it out, they said, and the car will appear like magic in the driveway. Within a few days, a Blue Holden JX 240 station wagon arrives, as promised. Kiwis drive on the left hand side of the street and the steering wheel is on the right, not the left. Oh well, we're used to it, after years of driving around London.

So far, everything is done with professional care. Lintas is a first-class operation.

A beautiful, modern home with elephant-sized windows that allow light to flood into the spacious interior, 292 Victoria Avenue is virtually the first choice; it's a diplomat's home. The back garden is filled with lemon trees. Everything is big, including the dual lane stairway that sweeps to the second level. Going to bed is a scene from *"Gone with the Wind,"* with Scarlett O'Hara begging us to join her on the second level of her southern mansion.

Vicky Avenue, as Victoria Avenue is called, is a "pluty" (a contraction of the word plutocratic) neighbourhood with an orderly parade of neat Victorian homes perched along each side. The street

runs up a gentle rise from the harbor, leading to Remuera Road where it terminates. Most houses are white gingerbread; all are large homes for the rich and industrious of Auckland society.

Remuera Road crosses the top of Victoria Avenue, like a T. This is a small town, with a main street filled with lively shops and restaurants. Our favourites are the toy stores and a little shop full of dairy products and spicy meats. On Saturdays, the family strolls up the slope to buy fresh New Zealand cheeses, pepperoni and oven-fresh bread from the baguette across the street. We spend many happy days visiting shops, like Mr. Magic, the antique shops and furniture stores while watching prosperity walk by. Dining out takes place at Pinks, Boodles and other fashionable eateries. Everest conqueror Sir Edmund Hilary also calls this part of Remuera home. And it is also home to New Zealand's most famous private school for boys, King's College, founded in 1896. King's provides the best education possible for the privileged of Remuera society. David and Anita Murphy's son, Matthew, is enrolled in this esteemed academy.

Within a few days we are experiencing a transformation from middle to upper class, and it's easy, *"when you live in Remuera."*

On Sunday morning, the air crackles with the sweet-smell of honeysuckle and summer rose. Church bells peal in the distance, sprinkling old-world sounds on our summer Christmas card. It's quiet, too, because everything is closed on Sunday; no business is conducted on the Lord's Day. Dogs don't even bark.

While landing at the airport a few days earlier, the traveler next to me said, "Turn y'er watch back fifty yeers mate. Y'er landin' in New Zealand." I didn't think much about it at the time, but within a few days I began to appreciate its meaning. We're trapped in an innocent cocoon from the past, prompting sweet memories of childhood. We feel safe walking the streets. The Pacific breeze is refreshing and saccharine. Neighbours stop leisurely strolls to welcome us and have a chat. Oh, life is so full of promise.

The children, too, fall in love with this sugared-land.

Our spirits are lifted by the sound of children laughing; the sight of dappled sunlight dancing along green hedgerows, while children skate and run bare-foot along the pathways. As it's the Christmas break, we discover school is closed until the end of January.

Yes, we know our daughters will grow strong in an environment like this, without the nasty blows of harsh weather, and a competitive society pushing them everywhere but where they want to go. Beverley and I quickly embrace the little things, like walking the children up the slope to the IGA to buy a Tip Top ice cream.

By the end of the month, daughters Michelle and Nicole are enrolled in a treasure of learning, just behind our house, called Victoria Avenue Primary School, number 252. Before they start school, neighborhood friends playfully mock their Canadian accent. Oh, how quickly they become Kiwified, as ten became "tin" and six became "sex." Living in Remuera also means they're to avoid using working class words like "cobber" (a friend), "cadge" (to borrow), or "bickies" which means biscuits, crackers or cookies.

Their first day at school, the teachers suggests we visit Waitangi on the northern tip of New Zealand, so the children will understand their history. Appreciating Waitangi is big in New Zealand; somewhat like Canada Day at home.

Each morning children stroll down the walkway to class "barefoot." No need for shoes, as the journey is like walking on clean sand. The girls all wear the same powder blue dresses. And there is no need to stand outside the school waiting to walk them home: they're safe, despite their tender ages of six and eight.

We're also pleased that David and Anita Murphy live a stroll up the "pluty" street, and the advertising agency is nearby in glitzy Parnell, a short five minute drive from our new imperial palace on Victoria Avenue.

Prime Minister Robert Muldoon

What country in the world would call its Prime Minister "Piggy", an affectionate nickname slapped on Prime Minister Robert Muldoon of the National Party? Yes, he does look a little like a sow. The citizens are so close to their beloved leader, Mr. Piggy. And I can't think of another country in the world that calls its parliament building, "The Beehive," it's practically an oxymoron. This is where Mr. Piggy works, in the capital city of Wellington. And imagine a country with a turnout of 91.4% at election time.

New Zealand Parliament Building

Thousands of years earlier, the Polynesian settlers called it Aotearoa, meaning *Land of the Long White Cloud*. The current name, New Zealand, was burned onto a world map by Dutch explorer Abel van Tasman in 1642. He called it Nieuw Zeeland, after the Netherlands province of Zeeland. The British finished polishing their new crown jewel by calling it New Zealand. Even the name New Zealand is sweet and a promise of something new.

By January 14, I'm settled, have learned a bit about the country, and it's time to drive to the office and get to work.

Getting "Down-Under" to Work

The first few days at the agency are awkward. Unlike my sizeable Toronto office, everything is small, temporary and rickety. The workmanship looks as if someone's uncle did the handy work. It smells like a federal employment office: B.O. and tired smoke, with most staff grazing about, reading papers, and not being very talkative. Nor is anyone smiling. There is no evidence of hustle, or curiosity about the new arrival.

The staff, while friendly, seem to lack fire in the belly, and undoubtedly with David away had fallen into a torporific state. That is simply a first impression. Most arrivals, whose names I don't know, fall through the front door, looking dazed while gripping a morning pick-me-up. Perhaps they are just shy?

As a foreign invader, I know I will be tested and if I don't deliver soon they'll freeze me out. That's the way it is in most foreign countries when heavyweights arrive to replace local talent. They don't like it, and I will not fault them for thinking that way.

Two creative staff finally say hello.

Dutch art director Peter de Beer is quiet, gentle, but, I'm told, he likes his beer. The problem with Peter is he's an extremely talented "designer," but he's not an ad agency art director.

An agency art director has to design ads that force readers to follow logical steps when they glance at an ad. Headline first, then the message to sell the product, the product's name, finally, where to buy it. It's a hard discipline. A designer, on the other hand, creates beautiful images and colour to be enjoyed by the mind.

The other creative person I meet is another gentle art director, Terry Hall. My, he's such a nice man, and the only Maori in the office. Give him a pen and he can draw anything. He's one of the best I've ever worked with: he's a visualizer, he can draw brilliantly, but he's not an art director in the modern agency sense. One of the habits Terry has is "taking a walk-about" from time to time: disappearing and not returning for a few days. Staffers say it's a

Maori tradition and I should get used to it. I do.

So, I have two challenging art directors who will ultimately have to change their ways if we are to become an advertising agency.

Within a week, my first impression changes as work they've done surfaces. It is excellent.

The slower pace and an untraditional skill-set is producing some powerful results. A previous creative director, since moved back to Wellington, produced brilliant work with this same team. So I begin to appreciate that this talent pool is different, but I too can probably get good results.

The critical change I have to communicate is that they must create ideas, not ads, or TV commercials; just ideas that will turn people on.

Within a week, I've concluded, I must do what I've been trained to do: crank up the productivity and lead by example, nothing more, nothing less. No one noticed my initial disappointment, so I jump in the saddle and head toward the future.

New Faces Jump on Board

New faces begin to appear. Murphy hires an additional three to improve the skills in the ranks and that's promising. It seems he is hiring highly skilled people in many departments from the world's ad-pool.

An associate creative director arrives and joins us at the office. Michael Forde hails from London, where he worked as a senior writer with Butler Dennis and Partners. Before that, he worked in Hong Kong, Rhodesia, and South Africa. Great personality and a talent that will fit into the jigsaw puzzle to improve the fortunes of the Auckland office.

Account service is also beefed up. A critical part of the agency operation that bridges relations between client and agency. Aside from keeping clients happy, with sound strategic advice, they make sure the accounts they manage are profitable.

Tim Roberts is the first to hop on board. He's another Brit, joining from USP Needham in Australia. Tim is a footballer if there ever was one, short and muscular with a body a car would bounce off: a bubbly sort of man everyone will like immediately. Tim, too, worked in the UK. We immediately get to know his wife Diana and the kids. He will be handling the dicey Smith and Nephew account, with a worldwide skin-care brand familiar to all: Nivea.

Finally, a production manager is added: David Russell from Gray Scott Inch, where he's been employed for more than four years. Russell is known as the sharpest production pencil in the country. About thirty-eight, 5 foot 6 inches, solid slim build with a chipmunk smile, Russell has a tight face and a hairline that's racing back toward balding. Nice, honest, a friendly type with two kids and a lovely wife. Russell also lived in Toronto for a while, but was driven out by old man winter. He has eighteen years experience, including eight in Canada and Europe. That endearing smile makes him a cool negotiator when getting production quotes, a skill that's a terrific asset right now for Murphy's team.

Lovely black-haired Nicole Smith from Wellington is one of my first creative additions. Nicole is training to be a producer, to take charge of a mass of television and radio campaigns, and she does. She's a wisp of a girl. Doesn't smile, but her cool demeanor makes my heart race.

Lintas, in short order, is attracting excellent people, and in such a hurry. The spirit in the agency is gaining momentum and the banter is free-wheeling and encouraging. A spark has been lit and it's evident Lintas Auckland is on its way somewhere.

Good advertising accounts with good products to sell are the lifeblood of successful agencies. At Lintas, we have a few "great accounts" for sure.

If the agency is worth its salt, it must provide good marketing and advertising advice to its clients, and it must create advertising and media plans that actually sell products to customers. Success is measured by *"sales results"* or changing how people think about a product. If they feel better about a product after a campaign runs, that is a positive thing. Customers might buy the product next time. That's pretty simple stuff on paper, but difficult to achieve.

The more I look about, the more I realize Murphy's team has done above average work. In fact, it has achieved remarkable results for most clients. But he is determined to do better. That's what inspires him to reach out to his bosses in Paris and London to get their agreement on adding more experienced staff and international muscle to his team line-up. It appears someone is listening.

The reporting procedure is important. But in Murphy's case, it's a little odd. He reports directly to Jean-Francois Lacour, the co-

Jean-Francois Lacour

ordinator for the region who lives in Paris. As part of the global order, he's the point man responsible for Asia and the South Pacific. Lacour is an accomplished advertising man, with a brilliant grasp of the English language. Sydney office had the pleasure of his leadership for three years prior to Bruce Harris. The problem with Lacour is that he's on the road at least ten months of the year, rarely settling back into his Paris office, while reporting to Lintas International in London. Communication can become a problem. After all, an Englishman, with a Kiwi burr, reporting via telex to a flying Frenchman dashing from airport to airport, office to office, while issuing reports to London, is not the easiest way to pass along subtle information on a regular basis.

The Australian office, under the leadership of Harris, also reports to Lacour.

Hopefully, the recent agreement by Lacour to add staff in Auckland will propel the operation to the top league in New Zealand. After a few weeks, it's apparent Murphy is on his way and has not taken a misstep.

The biggest and most profitable accounts, which demand the most staff time, are a carpet company and a cookie manufacturer.

The carpet company is the largest producer of all-wool quality carpets in the world. It's enormous and successful selling its wares to retailers and stockists in New Zealand and Australia. This is our biggest international account. I will soon get to know the name Feltex, a brand little known outside of the South Pacific region and the worldwide carpet industry. New Zealand has forty-five million sheep, with one born every minute: it's no wonder Feltex is located here.

The other major player is a cookie and cracker company, producing products sometimes referred to as *bickies*. There is no doubt its produces some of the finest brands in New Zealand. Aulsebrooks is the name, but it manufactures and markets worldwide brands, like Huntley Palmer.

The work the agency is doing on these accounts is truly spectacular and a hard act to follow. The work done by the local team would test the brain cells of the finest in any market. Surprisingly, it is not recognized as great stuff. During the early days at the office, I often question why they need me, other than for the comfort of my North American "accent" and international experience, which locals might find appealing.

There are many other clients, mostly local, some international, but relatively small. We believe all of them can be developed over time and that is encouraging. Some will become world brands in the decades ahead.

The other business that demands my attention is simple: *buying gas* for the car. It just so happens there's a British Petroleum, or BP, station on Parnell Road that I pass on my way home to Victoria Avenue.

Not a big deal, but a routine I must follow every seven days, as my Holden seems to enjoy a belly full of gas.

Little Blue People Walk Into My Pocket

Within minutes of leaving the agency parking lot, and motoring up a slick road, I pull into BP, just a plain gas station with a friendly and efficient staff. After filling up and paying the bill, in cash, I receive a special gift from the attendant.

A little blue thing, like a small man wrapped in clear plastic, is thrust into my hand. The pretty attendant smiles, laughs, and says something I never understood, implying that I'd won something and, oh gosh, I should be so happy. "What the guts is: dey're free. Cheery bye," she said.

Obviously, I'd missed the big promotional sign over the entrance saying FREE SMURFS. How would I know they're giving something away, I can't even say the word: Smurf.

These hard rubber critters are about two and a half inches tall, and look like little blue cartoon people. The one I am given today is holding a feather in one hand and has a scroll in his other hand. He's a writer, I think. His silly grin makes me laugh. The white hat on his head is similar to a Canadian toque. "*Yuk,*" I think, put it in my pocket and drive home. But when I show it to my daughters, they squeal with excitement, and celebration ensues. They've heard about these little critters from school and want to start collecting them. Their school friends didn't know where they came from either: they just seem to follow their parents' home.

Smurfs are a hit, and the only way I can collect them is by buying gas, or petrol, at a BP gas station. I'm hooked. So are the children. *"Hey Doddy, will you peeze buy more gaz?"* asked Michelle.

I also discover the Smurf you get is potluck: you get what the gas station has that day. So you might end up with a hundred Smurfs called "Writer Smurf", the first I collected, or you can buy gas for years until you collect *one hundred or more different little blue friends*. The more we stare at them, the more we enjoy these sociable little rascals. "How appropriate," I think, "a writer."

The history about Smurfs is soon discovered. They were created in Belgium by a cartoonist named Peyo. Soon, collectors realize the tiny Smurfs emulate all trades, moods and traits and shortly thereafter became a world hit. But, the creator's name is not really Peyo. That is a name given to him because no one outside of Belgium can say his real name: Pierrot Culliford. So, Peyo stuck and Pierrot lost his real name to history.

Now kids all over the world dream about owning Writer Smurf, King Smurf, Smurfette, Baby Smurf, Dark Smurf, Smurf and the Magical Egg, Astro Smurf, The Apprentice Smurf, Sleepy Smurf, Doctor Smurf, Wild Smurf, Reporter Smurf, Dreamy Smurf, Jokey Smurf, Handy Smurf, Lazy Smurf, Greedy Smurf, Farmer Smurf, Miner Smurf, Clumsy Smurf, Poet Smurf, Brainy Smurf, Nosey Smurf, Sleepy Smurf. You name it; there is a Smurf by that name.

In the days ahead, Smurfmania will sweep the planet, hitting distant lands like Bulgaria, Croatia, Denmark, Holland, Estonia, Finland, Germany Greece, Israel, Italy, Iceland, Korea, Sweden, Spain: the list is long, but doesn't include Canada.

The little German-made figures had become a phenomenal promotional item for British Petroleum stations while we were in New Zealand. Now, that's clever marketing.

Within a month, the children have Writer Smurf, two Baby Smurfs, two Smurfettes, the pretty girl with the long blond hair,

Dreamy Smurf and Nosey Smurf. Not bad for starters.

These little blue people will play a big role in the lives of the children and provide an entertaining diversion from the heavier days we'll have to face. And, there is a Smurf tragedy not too far ahead, involving over a hundred friends who get a ride home in my pocket.

Chapter 3

THE REWARDS OF SMART

The carpet account, Feltex, is king of quality. Hell, what else can you do with forty-five million Romney sheep grazing on land the size of Britain other than make carpets and export a lot of mutton and lamb chops? So, Feltex has a source of wool, right on its doorstep. The end result is that wool from Kiwi sheep make the most beautiful all-wool carpets, ready to be walked on in the finest hotels and the most sumptuous palaces for royalty and the titled. Even places like the United Nations, Buckingham Palace and the White House all have Feltex carpets somewhere in the buildings.

But they don't sell a lot of carpets to the average "Joe and Jayne" wanting to impress neighbors down the street.

Too expensive, say most people. Frankly, they prefer to walk on wooden floors. A carpet is a carpet as far as the average shopper is concerned. They don't want to throw money away buying quality just to impress neighbors. So Feltex plays in shallow water, until an idea from Lintas Auckland comes along.

This is a good example of excellent marketing, embracing the four Ps: product, pricing, promotion and placement.

David and the agency develop an idea that'll have monumental impact.

The idea is to create a "super-brand" of carpet to be fashioned by a designer with considerable international fame. This star designer will be the first chosen to endorse the new FELTEX INTERNATIONAL DESIGNER COLLECTION.

His face and giant cutouts of the man will be in all carpet stores.

He will be seen pointing to carpets, in colours and textures he has personally chosen. The designer will put his name on carpets that will appear in fashion-sensitive homes throughout the South Pacific. His signature will be on a gold band stitched across the corner of the carpet. What an impressive sight and what an impression it will leave with neighbors and friends. That's the theory. But would anyone pay big bucks to have a designer's name on a carpet installed in their home? The concept flies in the face of some unearthed market data, so it's daring. We're about to challenge old wives tales. Wrong, in this case, is right. People do want to impress (but never say it); they do want to cover up wood! That's the reason for the new product.

Feltex probably thought it crazy, too. First, how will a company in New Zealand attract the attention of a famous designer in Paris? Anyway, he'll cost too much money. No, it's crazy!

But enough research has been conducted to *indicate* that the idea has some merit and indeed will be attractive to homeowners in the South Pacific.

The result reflects the moxie and stubbornness of David Murphy and Lintas. Dream big, gamble and strut your skills on the big international stage.

Carpets from the "Wood of the Ship"

Within a few blinks, the Paris office helps us to sign him up and the idea is approved. *Pierre Cardin* has signed on to endorse the line and to lend his "haute couture" eye to the marketing challenges. A small royalty is agreed and payable to Cardin for every carpet sold. If the idea dies, his royalties will be nil. If it succeeds, everyone will benefit, especially Feltex.

There's little downside to the idea. After all, Cardin is not being paid a handsome hunk up front which could allow him to walk away if the idea bombs. The risk is shared in a surprisingly generous way. There is no way Cardin is going to associate his reputation with a second-rate operation. No, this means one of the world's greatest designers is endorsing Feltex.

Now we have to stop him long enough to film the TV commercials. After lengthy negotiations to capture Cardin on film, or just to capture a minute of his time, the gamble is ready to play out.

The Paris office of Lintas pitches in and a crew is dispatched to Paris to film the man waltzing through his introductory bits with style and élan.

Within weeks, the commercial airs and is greeted by dizzying cheers in the market place. It's a hit. There are a few exceptions, of course. Too *up-market* said a few disgruntled stockists.

Showroom material, newspaper and magazine advertising rush at the vulnerable consumer and they embrace Cardin's fashion product of the age.

What they don't know is that it's almost the same carpet that was previously available, but with a small band of silk sewn across the corner, hinting it has been designed by the magic man. Yes, it's a hit. The buzz is electric and the campaign oozes into Australia.

The advertising and promotional material is subtle but confident.

"Feltex of New Zealand, the largest manufacturer of woolen carpets in the world. And the world's most respected designers. Out of this unique partnership has arisen the birth of a new departure, a new elegance in carpet design: The Feltex International Designer Collection, a range of carpets in styles and colour that will complement today's tastes in décor – Pierre Cardin."

It's triumphed as the "Cardin Coup."

Yes, it's a mega hit, based on the global smarts of Murphy's team and Feltex. It's worth repeating. It's another example of the enormous risk-taking Murphy, his team and client are willing to take to leap ahead in New Zealand. And the idea itself is a big one that is scary and, most said, unachievable because of the enormous challenges. But it works.

The funniest part during filming of the commercial is hearing Pierre say, **"The carpet is made from the 'wood' of the 'ship' in New Zealand."**

His best attempt to say, *"from the wool of the sheep…"* fails miserably and he doesn't have the patience to say it correctly for English ears. In fact, he believes it sounds, *"…bien."*

Within a year, Feltex New Zealand had a record profit, as the ad campaign lifted sales and profit to record levels for the year ending June 30. Sales are up 22% to $444 million, including an increase in carpet exports of 29% to $57 million. The Auckland Star reports September 7, 1982, page 20, that net profit after tax rose 39% to almost $23 million New Zealand dollars.

A clever marketing idea and fearless and decisive leadership at Feltex by John Cameron made a major contribution to this success.

A TASTE OF HOME

The other celebrated success is our "bickie" company, Aulsebrooks, a legendary New Zealand market leader that has the smarts, and does its homework. It is big in New Zealand, like Christie's in Canada, Nabisco in the U.S. or Arnotts in Australia.

Aulsebrooks also relies on the talent pool at Lintas New Zealand for a number of new products it's bringing to market.

One of the new products is a "cookie" sold in a bulk bag, for kids who like to scoff 'em. But this cookie will *stay fresher* because it's in a foil-lined bag. After five years of research in markets around the world, Aulsebrooks knows shelf life is all-important and has a direct link to repeat sales and profitability.

The foil-lined bag means cookies will have four times the shelf life of cookies in clear cello-bags and a 60% better shelf-life than printed cello bags. And, mum won't have to put the cookies in a cookie jar to keep them fresh. She'll just scrunch up the foil-lined bag to keep them fresh. Goodbye, cookie jar.

But Aulsebrooks people are smart and decide to launch the campaign with big-sellers like chocolate chip cookies and shortbread, then expand the line if sales take-off.

"Positioning," a new marketing philosophy created by Trout and Reis, is just starting to hit home runs. It refers to where a mother will

"position" the new cookie in her mind. We want to own the word "fresh," so Aulsebrooks and the agency decide to explore the *"fresh – just like mum's homemade cookies"* positioning.

The name *"Farmbake"* is chosen and a promotional line is developed by the agency that says, *"Farmbake. A taste of home."* Mums with kids in an 8+-age grouping, will be the targets of our message.

It's also agreed that advertising on television and at point of sale will always show New Zealand schoolboys away from home at private schools, receiving cookies with a letter from home. The children will never reach home, because Farmbake cookies provide "a taste of home," and are just like cookies mum makes.

It is a colossal hit, for the oddest of reasons, to be discussed later.

One of the first challenges I am involved in for Aulsebrooks is simple, to design a commemorative biscuit tin to celebrate the wedding of Prince Charles and Lady Diana: the Camelot Royals adored by New Zealand families. This event is big news. The wedding is to be celebrated as a Royal fairy-tale romance in Commonwealth countries like New Zealand. It's the chatter by the tea-set and has created monumental opportunities for marketers of products that are somewhat related to the event.

My job is to design a tin to celebrate the wedding. It's a simple task; select a photo and place the date of the wedding on the front. It'll be a commemorative tin filled with the finest bickies from Aulsebrooks' bakeries.

This is a collectible that will be of immense value as an antique in the year 2081. The date, July 29, 1981, is wrapped about the circular metal container. Because Royalty souvenirs are so popular, it doesn't take long before the tins are gobbled up by collectors and mums wanting to commemorate the day.

Murphy and I soon realize we have chemistry that can turn straw into gold.

The tall, dapper Murphy is good at sniffing out new business opportunities in the marketplace, and that is critical. I didn't know a soul in the city and am incapable of smelling anything other than the whiff of beer from the Alexandra Tavern around the corner, where we go to get "streeted." Winning new business is really a matter of having contacts, sniffing around, asking questions, doing hard work, a little research and developing winning strategies to sell to business prospects. It also helps if the image of the agency is hot and it has a reputation for doing good work that sells products. One day the roll of the drums is heard: an account is looking for help so we jump on stage.

DTR is a television and VCR rental company that's big in New Zealand and the UK. In fact, it's the video rental leader, worldwide. DTR is proud to say it rents more than four million television sets around the world. That is some doing. Most householders in this country don't own a television set; they simply rent one, and the New Zealand division of this British company has done well in most parts of the country.

Boom, in the door we blast with what we believe is an earth-shattering idea. THE ANSWER IS YES: the campaign idea wins us more new business.

Television commercials, radio, newspaper and magazine ads will be prepared and on the air in days. Can we do it? The answer is Yes! The idea for the commercials is to have prospective customers sing a number of impossible requests. Then other singers respond with a resounding, *"DTR, DTR - THE ANSWER IS YES!"*

Classical versions are aired, appealing to the high-end of the market; pop versions for the teens, and country and western versions for others. Musically, we beat the drum, trying to appeal to every musical taste in the country and to every age group. Did it succeed? The answer is yes, as it's a totally integrated, simple idea that had the staff inside DTR feeling good. What consumers hear on radio is enhanced on television. What they hear or read in newspapers is repeated when customers visit the stores, scattered throughout the land. It's one voice, one message: whatever you expect from a TV rental company, you'll find it here. The answer is YES!

The one thing that struck us during the pitch is how effortlessly we work together and how comfortable we are with each other. We enjoy doing it because we're having fun.

Know the Market

It doesn't take long before we learn more about this exquisite kingdom and its extraordinary ways. By March 1981, the family is falling in love with the country and its easy going people.

The two big islands, north and south, have a population hovering around three million, with about a third, or one million, living in Auckland. Smaller than I thought: but it feels bigger.

New Zealand is referred to as "England in the South Pacific," and that is understandable when you look around. The green and rolling countryside reminds me of my early years in Surrey and Kent in England. But New Zealand does startle with amazing differences. On the south island are massive glaciers; on the north island, semi-tropical forests, smelly "rotten-egg" geysers, mud-volcanoes, rugged fiords, pristine lakes and forests with the occasional Kauri tree, the planet's hardest wood, now under resuscitation in protected reserves.

The land area is small, too, a mere 103,300 square miles, about the same size as Britain at 100,000 square miles. By comparison, Canada dwarfs New Zealand, with 3,560,238 square miles.

Wellington, the capital of this tiny perfect Dominion, is stuck on the bottom of the north island.

The brash commercial capital of Auckland calls itself boss. It's on the west coat of the northern island and is the country's fastest growing city.

About 90% of the main population is of British descent, although most were born here. The Maoris from Polynesia settled here first, some 650 years ago. They make up about 7%, with the remaining 3% a blend of cultures. It's a lovely mix of people who live happily on these tiny islands.

Access to television is primarily through Television New Zealand (TVNZ), formed in 1980, but still in government hands.

Radio is now free of government control. The new sounds emanate from stations like the spirited Radio Hauraki, New Zealand's first pirate radio station, founded in 1966. By the time we arrive, radio is real, with madcap disc jockeys like Blackie, welcoming us and cheering on the populace with commercial radio that Kiwis are quickly adjusting to.

The weather is pleasant all year round, particularly on the north island, where I'm located. Flowering-trees, scented flowers, shrubs and creepers are everywhere. If you stand still for five minutes clematis, forget-me-not or edelweiss will spring forth from the dirt between your toes.

There are no native animals, with the exception of a dinosaur we'll talk about later. But they have a variety of beautiful birds like the black and white tomtit, wrens and silver eyes. Lovely names, but they never sit long enough to let me take a picture. The craziest bird of all is the kiwi, which cannot fly but is so revered the people are named after it.

The one animal that now makes New Zealand home is an immigrant: the white fluffy sheep. There are six main breeds: Merino, Halfbred, Corriedale, Romney, Coopworth and Perendale, typically used for meat and by wool producers like Feltex. British colonists first transported sheep to the country in the early 1800s. It is said, with pride, that a new one is born every minute. For Kiwis, that's some achievement. But, who counts them? Lamb is another staple that has put this country on the world map as producers of quality foodstuffs from lamb chops to cheeses and other dairy products.

There are so many activities for the family. Whether strolling through Parnell's Rose Garden, the Auckland Lion Safari Park or the Auckland Domain Museum, it's always good family activity. The family visited an ancient volcano in the city center, now surrounded by even more sheep wandering the grassy bits. It's called One Tree Hill, because of a huge Totara tree that was perched on top until 1876. It was a landmark that could be seen for miles around, but is now gone. The hill had been inhabited from the 14th century until the middle of the 18th century by the Waiohua Tribe. It's very peaceful here. You can smell the fresh grass and the scented air. High blood pressure drops rapidly, even in the middle of a metropolis of almost one million.

Often, we have a barby on the local beaches on the Hauraki Gulf with Murphy and his family, or take short trips to historic settlements or the fairgrounds, to play on the 1960s Ferris wheel or merry-go-round.

Fitness, too, is an inherent craze. As well as running a few kilometers a day, I slip into cycling. Soon I'm doing five kilometers a day around the cycle trails of One Tree Hill. Did I feel good and fit? You bet. If I slowed down, Murphy's eldest son Matthew would urge me to, "Keep going, sir."

The agency also organized games of cricket, with agency players like Mike Howard challenging teams made up of clients. In a rare game, I'm awarded the title of "Most Entertaining Player," perhaps because I pitched the cricket ball too much like a baseball. It's lovely, though, sitting in the sun, on white deck chairs, on the greens, downing New Zealand wines while competing for the glory of being beaten by the clients. Perhaps we did give many wins away to ease the scowls of truculent clients, but that is what you are supposed to do, isn't it?

Beverley, an animal lover, decides to breed cats. Cats strike me as "big" here, compared to Canada. The New Zealand branches of the "felis domesticus" family make their Canadian cousins look like mice. The average local cat weighs at least fourteen pounds.

Within days, Beverley's in Penrose to buy a Burmese kitten. Renda Skikari is the name, the first purebred Burmese in our stable. But it's awkward shouting for Renda Skikari, so we name her Victoria, after the street we live on, and it sticks.

But before breeding kittens, we have to exhibit them to gain a reputation in a cat-loving society. That's the tough stuff: fluffing up and combing these beasts until they look beautiful for all of three minutes, while the judges inspect them. Before we know it, Victoria has won firsts, seconds, and special rosettes at the Franklin Cat Show, the National, the International Cat Show and the Takapuna "mog" Show. It's a wonderful diversion for my wife and a great joy for the children as they get to travel around the beautiful countryside seeing the best cats in the land.

It's so much fun that by April, it's time to find another cat to show and breed. This time it's to be purebred Siamese. Purelight April Lady arrives, another handle that's difficult to call out in the dark. As April is fool's month, her second name is April: April it is!

More cat shows, and the usual round of certificates and rosettes. It provides a release from the boredom and monotony that women in foreign ports often suffer. They've few close friends to console them, no relations to party with, while husbands travel around the region. It does take a toll on many marriages.

Because Beverley loves animals, she works as an assistant to Dr. Collin, a local veterinarian. She has finally found a replacement for her childhood years working with ponies and foals, competing in dressage events all over England. And now we have Dr. Collin to help maintain the cats' good health and good looks.

The children, too, have an interest other than playing with friends and their Smurfs. They now participate in the rearing of two very special cats that will soon become mothers.

Social life with the Murphys is now in full swing, not because we have to, but because we enjoy each others' company. Our respect for each other has strengthened along with the bond between our wives.

Anita is a wonderful, warm, straight-talking and attractive young lady. When she touches you, it communicates honest affection between friends. We enjoy each other's playfulness and often dream about what we might achieve together.

Murphy is more candid about his ten-year relationship with Lintas. His comments are usually complimentary or, at worst, humorous, as he regales us with stories of his many meetings in world cities during the infamous Lintas managing director conferences. It seems Murphy is more than a progressive: he's also a prankster who enjoys the excesses of life a bit too much.

Many years later, Bruce Harris recalled one incident.

"Murphy was a little drunk, and decided to lift another Lintas delegate's wallet while on a crowded Greyhound bus being driven back to New York after an international Lintas "live-in" conference in Connecticut. He stashed the wallet in one of the seat pockets in the bus, intending to retrieve it before he got off the bus.

Then in the middle of a farewell dinner at the New York Racquet Club, hosted by the Interpublic board for the Lintas visitors, he suddenly realized he hadn't retrieved the wallet when we left the bus. He quickly talked me into joining him to go back to the Greyhound Bus Depot down by the Battery to find the wallet. When we reached the depot, there were over 150 buses, all parked in a gloomy, cavernous bus park, all looking precisely the same. We started a desperate search, and, believe me; the first bus they let Murphy into... was the right one! Calculate the odds. And the funny thing is the victim that David chose, was Roger Neill, soon to be my successor in Sydney. I did notice similar characteristics in size, matching moustaches and general flamboyance. Years later Neill was able to manage the Sydney operation, while I crossed the Tasman for the Murphy Truman debacle."

May is upon us, and the weather has cooled as we approach a New Zealand winter. But it has not cooled enough that sailing is ruled out.

Friends in the neighborhood soon spring from the rich earth.

The Spring family lives next door. They have two children about the same age as our daughters and they have an Olympic-size pool, along with an enormous outdoor barbecue that would be the envy of Conrad Black. We spend many evenings and weekends at the Springs, just hanging out as we appreciated each other's company.

Other friends appear. Most are professionals, from doctors to lawyers to a pathologist and his family. The pathologist is Mark Jagusch. He and his pretty wife Colleen live around the corner, on

Sonia Avenue. Mark and nurse Colleen have three children, the youngest being Carolyn, about seven at the time, and two older sons, Brent and David. But Mark is also cursed because he's what they call a "yachtie." Aside from becoming close friends and being socially outgoing, they love to take us sailing in their thirty three-foot sailboat. Soon we're doing the yachtie thing aboard "Billbo Baggins," a name Mark disliked; sailing in Hauraki around dormant volcanoes, with legendary names like Rangitoto, Motutapu and Rakino, that dot the green seas that froth in the harbor.

Many weekends, we load up with fresh cheeses, sliced meats, oven fresh baguettes and bottles of New Zealand's finest white wines. Montana Sauvignon Blanc, a tasty "floral and appley" wine called Te Kiko, from Cloudy Bay, and a chardonnay whose label excites, because it promises tastes of "intense green fruit." The plan isn't to drink them all, just sample, and save the rest for the next barby by a volcano in the harbor.

Captain Jagusch would tack to the nearest volcanic island to anchor Billboa Baggins. Then, we'd board a small skiff and his oldest son David would row the short distance to shore. Once there, the children gather oysters and clams that cling to the rocks on the rugged beaches and begin the barbecue, Kiwi-style. By sundown, we are singing around an open fire until darkness ends the celebration, then we stare at the billions of stars straight above, trying to figure out the constellations, before beginning the romantic journey back to Auckland harbour. There is no life like it and sailing is soon in our veins.

Auckland Harbour

We celebrate Nicole's seventh birthday in a special way. A powerboat is spotted and we're determined to buy it as a surprise. Nicole has just begun to enjoy the seas. We tell the owner we want to test drive the powerboat on her big day, May 23. The owner pipes us on board our own boat we'll call *"Nicole"*, a powerboat I can handle with little training.

Within two minutes, the boat begins to sink, lower and lower into the water. Soon it's sinking so fast we must scramble off and cling to the pier. Within seconds it's been swallowed by the sea, much to the chagrin of the owner. The owner forgot to plug the water valves and with the extra weight, the open valves sunk the cruiser.

The water gods say you must NOT change the name of a boat. That must have been the curse that day: somehow they heard our suggestion.

On the way home, I'm low on gas. After looking for a BP station for a few miles, the tank begins gagging on the last few drops. Suddenly, a BP station appears ahead.

The reward brought joy to Nicole's pretty blue eyes, and lifted her spirits on her birthday. We'd finally found another Smurfette, the

pretty little Smurf with the long blonde hair and a pretty little dress. This one has pigtails and is wearing red roller skates. "Oh," I ask, "Is there more than one Smurfette?" "Oh yes *doddy*, there are *tin*," Nicole says, in her finest New Zealand accent. By now, Michelle has collected eight Smurfs and Nicole has ten.

And they know their names. Michelle has Smurfette, Pirate, Grouchy, Baker, Poet, Jokey, Slouchy and Greedy. Nicole has two Smurfettes, Baby, Snappy, Clockwork, Wild, Tracker, Astro, Aviator and Writer. We never know what happens to the little critters from day to day, because they take them to school to trade with friends. But, no one has KING Smurf and the hunt continues. What would life be like without our Smurf friends to take the curse away from the trials of everyday life?

The next day at the office, excitement is building, assignments are piling up and the engine is purring like an award-winning cat.

Chapter 4

SYDNEY AND KENNY

Bill Peake, the marketing manager of Aulsebrooks, shows up with a new cracker. To be precise, a prototype of a cracker from Huntley Palmer, a world famous brand name Aulsebrooks made legendary in New Zealand. But it's no ordinary cracker, it's completely different. And, they proudly claim, it won't be imported, it will be made at the Aulsebrooks cracker factory in Dunedin on the south island of New Zealand.

Peake explains, "There will be very little salt in this cracker." Salt is a thing of the past, because of the health scare. The big feature is: it snaps apart! You can have one big cracker with four parts, or you can crack it down the middle so you have two, or if you crack it again it makes two small crackers.

So there it is, lying on the boardroom table: no name, no reason to exist, no packaging and no personality. That's why the brand manager is at our door. Here's another opportunity for Aulsebrooks to make money.

This is the most challenging reason to be in the advertising business. Bring a dumb looking thing like this to market, and then give housewives a damn good reason to buy. At that time, women are responsible for 85% of shopping decisions in and around the home. They've got the power.

The top selling cracker in the market is Huntley Palmer's Cream Crackers, and Aulesbrooks is having sales success with a new Crispbread range (sort of like crusty bread); and now it has this new salt-free breakable cracker. It's a nice challenge, but it sure looks dumb sitting on a napkin in the middle of the boardroom table.

Within days a name is chosen: Crackits.

Naming products is often difficult, but if you've good people and think about the functionality and the benefit of the product, it's not difficult to create a short list of names. The rest depends on whether it looks and sounds right and can be easily remembered. Crackits sounds good: it's a snappy and descriptive name and it is not registered by anyone else. That, too, is a major challenge, as hundreds of names have been registered for future use by many competitors. So, Crackits it is!

It's tested in focus groups, with women who'll probably buy the product. The versatility and the salt-free approach makes sense to them. They like it.

Next, we develop a brand image, an advertising slogan and a brand personality that is different than anything else in the market place. The key is trial, or getting shoppers to try the new product. If they try it, it'll probably succeed.

The well-oiled Lintas Auckland genius flies into action. It's evident to all that the solution will be good, as confidence in the agency has grown enormously within a few short months.

A nautical theme is chosen and an idea borrowed from Gilbert and Sullivan. My father-in-law Charles Holland, in London, had spoken to me with wild excitement about Gilbert and Sullivan's two act comic opera, "The Pirates of Penzance," a smash hit when it opened in New York on New Year's Eve, 1897 and ritualized by opera companies around the world. Everyone knows *"The Pirates"* and many can sing much of the repertoire.

A colour is chosen for packaging and promotion. Seawater is a natural; blue, blue, blue. Everything went into production.

We have a personality, a name and now we need a slogan. Within a day we have the answer and because of the *Britishness* of New Zealand we believe it'll appeal.

It may be long but why not sing it in a Gilbert and Sullivan rhythmic meter, *"Crackits, Crackits, 4-2-1, Mansize-Snacksize-Bitesize crackers with a hint of salty air."*

That's it, they all scream. Brilliant, especially when sung with Gilbert and Sullivan's musical verve. And they love the *"hint of salty air,"* as women know men still want a whack of salt, but mum is

Snacker and Manton   *The Captain and Bitty*

trying to cut down. So the word "hint" is right-on-the-money.

After casting around, we find a terrific New Zealand animation studio that will create the look of the cartoon characters.

Next, we draw four cartoon characters to represent the stars in the television commercial. We have to draw the captain of the ship, then we have to create a big eater named *Manton*, who wants the big four-part cracker, then *Snacker*, who wants the medium-size cracker and finally *Bitty*, the young lady who wants the small, single portion. Now we have the ensemble cast, but we'll have to find a voice to bring life to the characters.

Once again we step beyond easy and choose Kenny Everett, a popular '60s disc jockey in London. Kenny Everett is one of pirate radio's first disc jockeys and has a worldwide reputation as an impressionist. We listen to his radio tapes and agree, *"He's the one!"*

"London?" Peake asks. "But he lives in London, why London?" Well, that's where he lives, we say. The clients finally agree to the idea and we arrange a recording session half a world away.

How can we be sure we can afford this comic genius?

We can't, but our office in the UK informs us that Everett is going to be in Sydney soon. "Aaaaah," we scream. It's nothing but bloody luck!

Everett is perfect. I spoke to him briefly, gave him a verbal brief and within seconds he's singing all four voices over long distance phone lines. "Sensational," I said, and rush to Sydney to meet with him at Bogtunes, a recording studio. The cost to get him to do the session is very low, as he knows the market is small. As long as we pay him in cash, everything is OK. For Everett, it's easy loot for a few hours of work while on holiday in Sydney. Everyone wins when it all comes together like this.

Crazy Everett loves doing the voices. He then records a simple message of encouragement to be sent to all stockists and retail outlets with his version of what to do to sell the new cracker. *"Get out and sell this cracker, or I'll come over and snap your neck!"* he chortled on the recording. Kenny Everett has turned the recording into an hour long stage show, performing for everyone, falling over, dazzling a small recording studio audience at Bogtunes.

There's a moment when I thought he'd lost it, but somehow he manages to return to the script and deliver the appropriate words. Boom, boom, splash: it's another hit from the team at Lintas Auckland, which is now becoming unbeatable in the market.

The recording is a snap: Crackits is on its way to becoming a hit.

Everett singing, *"Crackits, Crackits, 4-2-1, the Mansize-Snacksize-Bitesize cracker with a hint of salty air,"* is replayed on our minds' ears, like a hit recording, throughout the production of the radio and television commercials.

What did catch us off-guard is something that happens all too often in the industry.

The dreaded product name change!

Kenny Everett recording in Sydney studio

Copyright problems block the use of Crackits as a brand name, after we've recorded everything. The budget has been exhausted.

Everett has returned to London. Everything has been put on tape and is edited together with the animation, ready to go to air.

The new name is *"Snapits!"*

Not quite as nice, but the crackers do make a "snap" sound, as well as a crack, when you split them apart. So, Snapits is the new name.

For financial reasons, there is only one decision I can make, and that is to record the new name - *by doing it myself!* I did my best to sound like Everett. Nervously, I sat in the booth and every time Everett said, "Crackits," I would insert, "Snapits." The end recording is a testament to recording engineers and technology, not to me. They insert the new name into the existing voice track, take the old one out and no one ever knows, except me, the engineer and the client.

If marketplace sales are all that matter then the campaign is a success as headlines in *Marketing Magazine* in February of 1982 reported, *"8% at a "snap."* And one of the reasons is that, *"The most redeeming feature of this Snapits commercial is the strong brand personality of the Captain. This positioning strategy has taken the commercial out of the "me-too" trap which is a problem with biscuit type advertising."*

The new sales-team

Zing, another winner is launched and succeeds, but I'm advised the Lintas world is not paying attention. Our early successes are being ignored. These are remarkable achievements that should be reported in *Advertising Age* or *Strategy*, two of the great global marketing magazines.

LOSING WITHOUT EVER LOSING

When you're on a roll, nothing can stop you. Advertising people know "winning" is like a drug: it has an impact on your mind-set and strengthens the confidence of the agency team members in themselves. They believe they can do no wrong and for a time, they can't.

The agency pitches account after account that is looking for help. When Murphy and I breeze into a meeting, having done our homework, we exude confidence and it's catching. Like the great plague, the gale sucks up the prospect, who is suddenly blown along with it.

Bendon, one of our first new business wins, is a Kiwi icon, a highly successful company that designs and markets lingerie and men's underwear (referred to as grunds by rough-house Kiwis). It's a funny account. We probably never understood what they were trying to do and I'm not sure they did, but they are innovators. They provoke change and are willing to gamble if poked and prodded.

That's what we were good at and probably what we did best.

A Bendon brand that is memorable is called "Fellas," a stylized men's brief both skimpy and skintight: so stylish that many said only "poofters" would buy them. Fellas came in a variety of bright colours and a very slim cut. It certainly is the shock underwear for machos, stepping out of Y fronts.

We know *who* to target, and it *isn't* the presumed buyer: the man or the teen. No, it's *women*. Yes, women, and girls who buy for their men, as it seems men don't buy underwear. In most cases, it's the girlfriend or the mum. They want their men to look cool and stylish, and they see an opportunity with "Fellas."

But first we have to talk to the stockists and retail stores that will sell the Fellas line. If we get their agreement, it'll be fairly easy to reach our target group of women. But we don't have a big budget, either.

After a lot of animated discussion, we have an answer.

The strategy is to get the underwear talked about, as WOM, or word-of-mouth advertising is the most effective and least expensive form of getting the message out. But, it's hard to get talked about. The market has seen everything, and underwear is near the bottom of the yawn category. The media recommendation is radio and outdoor billboards in Auckland. That's about all the client can afford.

When we pitch for the business, we don't really care if we win or not. What we want to do is present a campaign that is daring and *will work:* that is all that matters to us.

A brash campaign theme line, *"Get 'em off,"* is written and a jingle is recorded in London, England. Why London? Hell, we want a sound from the future, no matter where it comes from in the world.

The music people phone back within a few days and play it to us.

The jingle sucks: it's twenty years ahead of the market, like orchestrated chain saws. So, we re-create it in Auckland with a local genius. By now I realize New Zealand's talent pool can deliver everything. Why go abroad for talent when it's just down the street?

Then, we photograph a muscular male model wearing all the styles of underwear and slam close-ups of his mid-section on huge billboards, with the "Get 'em off" theme. It's to be in your face when you walk by. We insist the billboards be placed at sidewalk level so anyone walking by will be encouraged to write graffiti on them.

And they do, drawing the occasional penis sticking out from the underwear and scribbling crude remarks like, *"Only poncers - get em' off"* and every other disgusting thing pranksters could think of to deface our hoardings.

The client didn't realize this is part of the strategy. We *want* this to happen. We hope local newspapers will report the incidents and show photos of disgraced billboards in the news sections.

They do, and *word-of-mouth* advertising works its cerebral magic, as the noise created contributes enormously to the success of the rebel brand. At least, we hope so.

The unexpected kicker is that a lot of women bought the underwear for themselves, as it became a unisex brand for a while.

Little did Lintas know that Bendon, founded in 1947, would soon become a global lingerie giant, with offices in the USA, UK, Australia and New Zealand, and could be a prospect account for the international offices of Lintas. Why don't they think ahead, and promote our successes instead of looking only at work done by their big offices?

Lintas reports the success in its own international paper, only because we sent photos and screamed about the success of a wild new fashion, but nothing more is said. No congratulatory notes, just silence. It's reported only because we sent the editor a provocative photo of a nearly naked model with the press release. By now, I know how they think. But they never knew what we were thinking.

The agency is still a cauldron of excitement, determined to win recognition in the region.

Spalding is another familiar brand that jumps on board. They market everything from golf clubs and balls to tennis rackets and skis. The dynamic team pitched for the business and scored another hole in one.

The challenge for golfers at the time is to find their balls on the course. They're all white and confusion reigns supreme. Spalding introduces golf balls in bright day-glow orange and green colors. The theme for the Spalding Hot-Dot-Optic-balls is easy: *"Distance with relief in sight."* The hits just keep rolling along.

Nivea, run by Brit N.P. Hamley, another world famous brand and a company struggling in New Zealand asks for help.

The first challenge is to improve sales of Nivea Cream Soap, a unique moisturizer soap bar for women.

The recommendation is to shift distribution of the product from supermarkets to "chemists." The solution came easily: a five-minute solution and a marketer's dream solution. Remember, one of the 4 Ps in successful marketing is placement, or what we call distribution of the product. This solution is the first of the 4 Ps. And the fix is our first clever move.

The advertising slogan, *"The only soap bar that'll give your skin a drink,"* is plastered on handsome display material to be placed in drug stores across the country. It's clever promotional stuff, but the marketing trick to change distribution is the critical part of the solution. All of a sudden, the bar is selling fast. After four weeks, sales have exceeded budgeted figures and show an upward trend. The *marketing solution* again made David Murphy look like a smart man in a tiny market, not showing up on the radar screen at head office. Instead they're probably looking at Australia, our nearest neighbor, for leaders with pixie dust. At the time, I shook my head at this simple solution. I had met few in Toronto, London, Paris or Brussels that have his talent. Murphy is a clever marketing man, not just a smart advertising man. There is a big difference, and it appears no one knows this, with the exception of the team in Auckland.

Like the bright child who tries so hard to get recognition from parents, I believe he became mischievous on international junkets just to get attention. And this is obvious to me six months into my tenure.

The next new business conquest is Thorn EMI; another global giant that markets quality TV sets. The account is won with considerable ease because we've perfected a style and a sense of ease that exudes authority and confidence in whatever we suggest. Contagious, too, as everyone absorbs the suggestions and responds with enthusiasm. I believe if we said shit is pink, they'd agree and applaud. Rarely has making presentations been so easy and so much fun.

Then we pitch Club Med, thinking, this is a lost cause. But it isn't. Soon, we have a crew on location at a Club Med, sucking up the dalliances of this sexually provocative French resort. Club Med at the time is seen as a French dream where singles go to enjoy sexual freedom under the sun.

It seems every new account we present an idea to gives us its business. There are no losses, only gains. The agony for Murphy is that the powers in Paris, London, New York and Australia, although informed, do not respond with praise or encouragement for the team or its leader at the helm in Auckland.

By now, I believe the conductor is restless; he wants to lead: he doesn't want to be led. There are hints he believes he will only achieve success by being on his own. Even the Wellington office seems to regard Murphy with suspicion. I believe it might be jealousy, envy or fear, as Wellington office doesn't seem to produce the high caliber marketing solutions Murphy is demanding. Yes, Lintas Wellington office produces good advertising, but not clever marketing ideas. Of the four critical Ps, they do outstanding advertising, but that seems to be the end of their capability.

I know Murphy is deeply troubled by the lack of regular response from Lintas and one day will just bolt, and this concerns me.

His discussions with Lacour seem to stop; perhaps Lacour's regional responsibilities just overwhelm him; maybe he is spending too much time with detail better left to an assistant he just doesn't have. Nothing matters anymore to Murphy, as the inspiring leader he has looked to in the past falls silent.

Moving with the Times

By winter, more office space is needed. It's time to make a statement about the maturity and dynamics of the business and it's accomplished in an unusual way.

The big dream is to become one of the three top agencies in the country. That's our objective, but it'll mean a 500% increase in business gains to reach number one. Our stubborn zeal says we can do it.

A Lintas billboard in Parnell has existed for some time, allowing us to poke fun at the competition. But they retaliate and deface it from time to time. It's nothing other than good-natured fun and intra-industry rivalry that shows a respect for Lintas. The reaction also trumpets the spirit and competitiveness of a booming industry in the country. But we also know we've outgrown the lunacy of Parnell and need to make a statement about stability and maturity. So we decide to move up.

At the end of May 1981, we move to the new center of the universe, Greys Avenue in downtown Auckland.

Greys Avenue is a wondrous old street, bristling with mature oaks and stately Georgian structures. The street runs downhill from Pitt to Queen Street, the main shopping avenue, and then rushes down to Auckland Harbour. Part way down Greys is this stately, three-storey estate from another era. It could be in Paris, or London. The exterior is white plaster, with velvet-green shutters, like butterfly wings fluttering on twelve generous windows that face the street. Additional dormer windows peak from the third floor roof line. An attractive entrance invites visitors to pass through green doors with big brass knobs. A white portico arches over the front doors, with fluted columns along the sides. The agency has landed. The warmth of success and presence is felt when you walk through the front doors. The agency is not looking back, we're marching forward.

On June 1, invitations to an open house are delivered to current and prospective clients. Additional business opportunities will surface; attracted by the smell of success and the celebrity we have gained. With a team working like a Swiss movement, the only fear is that something will go wrong. Lintas Auckland cannot lose a cog, or a beat, with such finely tuned talent operating as one.

Therefore, growth by adding the right people is what matters. When extra cogs are placed in the machine, they must complement the dynamics of this finely-tuned team. One badly hired person could disrupt the mechanism that is running faultlessly.

That evening when I arrive home, I'm greeted by the news that our first litter of kittens has arrived. Victoria, our award-winning Burmese, has given birth to a litter of seven cute little ones. One of the kittens, "Suchard Chantilly," is so beautifully proportioned Beverley decides to keep her as a future competitor.

Within months, the instinct is perrrr-fect as "Tilly" too begins to harvest awards and rosettes from the National and Takapuna Shows. The name selected is simply half of her official name, Chan-*tilly*.

For the first six months, everything is perfect and life for the family is moving along splendidly. The only dark cloud, aside from the winter sky, is mutterings from Murphy about his future. As he continues to indicate Lintas isn't listening anymore. Or maybe Murphy's a fanatic, one who can't change his mind and won't change the subject. He mutters, but no one is listening.

Chapter 5

NO, NOBODY'S LISTENING

THE SQUEAL OF TIREDS

Murphy never complains out loud about his masters and certainly never proffers his views to clients. It's personal: an escalating war of views with Jean-Francois Lacour about his future with Lintas. I believe him: I agree that no one is listening, not realizing Lacour is having difficulty with personal matters.

From Murphy's point of view, it's easy to understand his frustration after all he's been with the company ten years. In our business, it's rare to have a ten-year career with a single agency. He began in 1971 as an account director in Wellington, without a written contract of employment. On December 14, 1976, he was made a director of the company and put in charge of the entire New Zealand operation, as managing director. But there was still no written contract of employment, nor a written definition of his role. Evidence confirming these facts is provided by Bruce Harris at the trial after the formation of Murphy Truman.

Therefore, by appointing him to head up the country, it's evident someone thought he had the smarts. But who?

Murphy doesn't want much, just appreciation for his successes and a wage adjustment as he appears to be making less than me. His income is about $46,000 per annum, plus benefits, which is not a lot considering I'm on a $50,000. package. What he is asking for is relatively simple: he wants the company to pay his wages to a partnership formed by him and his wife. That might take financial pressure off the household and reduce his taxes. This arrangement is a standard business practice all over the world. What's wrong with that? Nothing, as everyone else seems to be doing it. My wage is paid to a partnership called Truman Associates, with Beverley and me as directors, so why won't they do the same for him? Do they believe he will not leave, when he's at the top of his game? New Zealand continues to be ignored, despite the huge new business gains of late and the successes with stable clients. It's a significant factor in his fanatical anger and the closer I get, the more I sense he's being shafted.

Relief from rumblings is needed about now, as word of the problems with Lintas reaches my wife. As we're surrounded by water, the solution is obvious: get sailing.

In July 1981 we're sailing on a regular basis in and around the harbor. Riding the waves with best friends, the Jaguschs, is now a habitual weekend activity. Mark and his wife Colleen are all bubble, the pinnacle of sparkling New Zealand company. They glitter with fun-to-be-with social chatter. Their children get along with our daughters, creating a bond of friendship that lasts for years. We load up on heavenly fresh breads, country cheeses and by now *boxes* of fine New Zealand wine and sail to the volcanoes. Boxed wine is the big thing, and we particularly enjoy the big green Montana Chardonnay.

I'm learning a little about the mainsail, leech tails, the jib, leeward and windward and a skill called "reading the luff." Defined as watching how the wind blows this tiny sail about at the front of the sail boat. It's the first indication of wind change. This is my job when helping Mark to navigate in heavier sailing conditions. So I'm doing my best to read the luff and report early wind changes back to the captain, by screaming wind changes to Mark.

Once anchored near a volcano, we lower the small skiff and his eldest, David, rows the smaller children to the shoreline of the volcano. The children jump out and run up the sides of Rangitoto and then run down the grassy interior of the volcano looking for bits of wood and little things that have washed down from the heavens. Then with David in charge, they trek back, reminiscent of a paragraph from "Lord of the Flies," to the black volcanic beaches ready to fire-up the natural barby. Within minutes shuck-ready oysters, bangers and pork chops are thrown on the hot embers for another feast on the beach. After the feast under the South Pacific skies, it suddenly turns black as big, overweight clouds roll in and it is time to head home. On this winter's day that started with such promise, we return through gale force winds as the enormous craft cut a swath through angry cross-waves, as it heaves us back to shore.

The luff is tossed around so much that day it gave up. Michelle, clinging to a door below deck, suddenly lost her grip and is thrown to the other side of the galley. Fortunately, she landed on a soft couch with big, fluffy pillows. Nicole and Carolyn are feeling a little sick; Brent and David are fine; Beverley is a fine shade of green. But with a little Montana from a box, it's an exhilarating ride to port. What more would be needed to relieve the stress of a week's folly?

Despite the successes and the move to new premises, Murphy's recent quiet spell signals trouble. When he's talkative things are fine. If he turns inward and remains quiet, it usually spells trouble. I know I have to get more involved.

The family celebrates July 1, Canada Day, in unexpected style. I mailed a letter to Prime Minister Pierre Trudeau some weeks back, asking if the Canadian government could send a large Canadian flag, as I'm unable to find one in New Zealand. A parcel arrives, in fact a large parcel, containing an enormous Canadian flag, hundreds of little flag pins and other trinkets to help celebrate Canada's birthday.

But the biggest surprise came a few days later. A secretary from the Canadian Consulate in Wellington called, saying they've been instructed to supply a Canadian Mountie in scarlet tunic for our Canada Day party in Auckland. What a shock, when the tallest, postcard Mountie appears on our doorstep.

It is a wonderful gesture by Mr. Trudeau and not the first act of kindness by the Canadian government while I've been posted abroad.

A MOVE TO RAMA RAMA

About now, David and Anita Murphy decide to move to a larger home, a move I never understand, considering his ongoing disagreement with his boss. After looking around for a while, they settle on what I call "Ponderosa" or the Old Coach Homestead on Kearns Road in Rama Rama.

The Ponderosa is a beautiful suburban property on ten acres of land in south Auckland. It's big, really big, just like in the television show.

Old Coach Homestead used to belong to a potter. An outdoor pool is in the rear, with wrap-around views of the rolling countryside. It will be an ideal place to entertain clients. Perhaps the Murphys believe he has arrived and it's time to make a dramatic move upward.

Their new home has an enormous country kitchen and plenty of room to breathe, no matter where you wander: five bathrooms, at least four bedrooms and a 600 square foot wine cellar. The house was built in 1976, and is about five years old when the Murphys purchase it.

The Old Coach Homestead is the place where we will celebrate many times, from Christmas right through every imaginable excuse to have a party. The new home isn't purchased because David and Anita came into sudden wealth; it is simply a time when they were probably feeling good about family life and believe they need to take the risk and move out of the city for fresh air and peace of mind. So they do. It is a hell of an investment, but maybe not for the Murphys short term goals.

(I believe they remained in the house until the mid-eighties, when they put it up for sale. The new owner remembers David asking, "What do you think?" after he showed it. The new owner said Murphy's business and marriage were on the skids, so he said he'd take it for half a million New Zealand bucks. Two and a half years later, it would be worth $1.5 million. It was increasing in value by about $4,000 a week. Mr. Bickerstaff, the new owner, did well, according to a report in the Sunday Star, July 5, 1987)

DRINKING, WOMANIZING & PLAYING AROUND

Anyone managing a multi-national office is aware of the dreaded visit by head office, to look at the books and talk about future plans. In Murphy's case, it's a final chance to talk face to face about grievances and how they can be resolved.

Well, that's not what some do. After all, these flying visits offer a chance for visitors to play away from home. Some arrive, eat and drink, maybe play golf, ogle the girls on staff and spend a few days in a bordello. If I hadn't experienced it, I would say it didn't happen. But sure enough, a representative arrives in August, does little, says little, but enjoys dribbling on foreign pillows, much to the delight of the local twilight girls.

His contribution to improving the efficiency and effectiveness of the office is nil, zero, blanko! I'm not sure he even knows where he is. To me, he stumbles around in a daze, with a smile on his face, most of the time. Spends a few hours looking at the books in search of something, and then boards the big bird to head home again. I don't know what is said to Murphy or what they discuss, but it isn't satisfactory.

Why is an individual assigned to manage global efforts, when in my opinion he should have been put to pasture years earlier? The task assigned to representatives is often beyond their area of interest. My anger is based on my view at the time and I suggest to Murphy that complaints should be addressed to someone higher up. His response is, "Right. To whom?" Nobody higher up will listen. There is no one else in London to talk to, and that has been his problem for some period of time. Playing politics with the powers at the helm of the big conglomerates is a deadly game. You usually lose, no matter how right you might be. The only opening he has is to quit and get out through the front door with pride intact.

Whatever transpired during those few days had dramatic repercussions leading to a final act that will soon be felt right around the world?

Murphy doesn't have to say anything after that. He finds it both troubling and career stalling and has no wiggle room left, as his final requests appear to be ignored. The frustration and anger have reached a boiling point. I know how diligently he works and how dedicated he has been. I agree he might be a bit of a rascal when attending global leaders' conferences. But who hasn't tied one on, or insulted someone, or been accused of pinching a bum?

Unfortunately, unknown to me, Murphy's reputation is widely known. One incident in particular has made the rounds and is recalled years later by Susie, a secretary at Lintas, Sydney. *"How could I ever forget David Murphy? You asked all of us to go out with him and take him to an evening show at the Hilton Hotel in Sydney where Shirley Bassey was performing and the only person who agreed to accompany him was Carol Casey. He got totally paralytic and stood up and called her (Shirley Bassey) a black and @#*&#, then attempted to molest Carol. She had the most frightening night ever and you apologized to Carol for years afterwards (for having) to put her through that…"*

Murphy is a lot of fun, a bit of a whacko, and can be impish if he's imbibed too much. But Murphy is also a loyal soldier and will be first to apologize if caught with his pants down.

I do not know how well the company has performed financially over the years. Blurring financial facts is a criticism hinted at by some at Lintas many years later. The Auckland office might not have been as profitable as head office wished, but I'm not sure. In the future, I will see evidence that David is capable of managing a bottom line and returning targeted earnings. He isn't afraid to gamble, not only with corporate money, but with his own money, as will be demonstrated.

In the meantime, the agency continues to barge ahead because of its brash nature and the promotional zeal in the genes. The creative product is hailed as different and effective, continuing a long tradition of excellence in a small market.

But Murphy is still smoldering and his attention is distracted from the bigger picture. By now, he's visibly shifting focus and that, too, is troubling. I'm sensing he has given up believing Lintas will help and is shifting his focus to a plan for setting up his own agency. I never believed it until this moment.

If he resigns suddenly, *I know my family will be caught up in the trouble* with no way of running back home. Auckland is the furthest point from home on the planet. Therefore, the cost of returning to Toronto is prohibitive. I also know the potential trouble ahead must to be kept away from my family, as I don't want an emotional meltdown when in fact a resolution, although distant, might still be at hand. But there are black days ahead. I don't want to remember them, because, *"I meant well, tried damn hard, but couldn't read the tea leaves."*

The lack of attention by Lacour from his office accommodation in Paris continues to be the big issue with both of us, and leads to numerous "talk and barf" affairs at the sticky-floored Alexandra Tavern in Parnell. The visit by a representative from the company paid no dividends; we are still wondering why they would send an emissary, supposedly ready to listen, but who ignored us.

The clients, however, treat us with ongoing respect and continue to introduce new challenges to keep our minds fit.

"Just like that!"

So it's back to our bickie account to keep us distracted while we prepare for the future.

The Huntley Palmer Digestive brand needs help and with the assistance of Tommy Cooper, the Welsh nut-bar with the red fez, we recommend a major television campaign. Cooper made the catchphrase, *"Just like that!"* popular at the time, so we use the same slogan to promote the cookie. Put anything from cheese, ice cream, or fresh fruit on top of a Digestive, and, as Cooper will say, "Just like that," it's a wholesome snack. The challenge is getting him to do it.

Tommy Cooper

Tommy Cooper, at sixty, has begun to slow down. Someone in London suggests we use an *impersonator*. No, we say, we want the real Cooper. They say no. Cooper agrees that we should use an impersonator. But, I say, a voice-over is all we need, so it should be easy. No, says Cooper, and he wins.

An impersonator records the script in London, while we listen and supervise by long-distance telephone. Talking to the impersonator is a gas; the guy sounds like Cooper even when ad-libbing with us. All is completed, in the middle of the night in Auckland. The voice heard on the television commercial is flawless, no one ever knows. *"Just like that,"* is a phony!

A report, *"Here's a little food for thought – 1981"* shows the volume growth of Digestive sales is 88% after eight weeks of heavyweight television advertising. Thanks, Cooper.

Tommy Cooper died three years later from cirrhosis of the liver. We all love Cooper and our wishes went to his wife Gwen, he called her Dove, and his children, Thomas and Vicky. A Cooper joke that I will always remember is, "Two cannibals are eating a clown. One says to the other, Does that taste funny to you?"

The point is made repeatedly that the Auckland office thinks big and takes enormous risk, while the Lintas network garners the accolades. Perhaps the greatest strength of the team is to dream big, think the undoable and take enormous risks. Perhaps that's a criticism that head office can point to. Thinking out of the box, at that time, is perceived as a weakness by many traditional agencies in Paris and New York.

Another marketing idea that went unnoticed is another of the green strokes by the team. Same client: Aulsebrooks, the country's most innovative bickie company.

It sells a variety of ordinary and boring tea biscuits with names like Super Wines, Round Wines, Vanilla Wines, Malt, Malt Meal Wafer, Butter Shortbread, Gingernut, Jamaica Wafer, Apricot Crispy and Lemon Dimples: ten different bickies with different appeals, for a number of small market segments.

The marketing idea is simple. Put all ten cookies under one NEW umbrella name, repackage them and promote the hell out of the bickies with one big budget, not ten little ones.

The name *"Teatime"* emerges as the winner and the repackaging begins, under the stewardship of the agency team.

Next we need an ambassador for the new brand, someone with star appeal and a personality that will appeal to women. We have a list of five potential people, but prefer one in particular.

After local research, our recommended name emerges as the winning choice: Pam Ayres, the internationally acclaimed comic, poetess and writer. She's a big name in New Zealand, with the "plain-sweet" biscuit-buying mums, the tea dippers. Ayres sells more of her books in New Zealand, per head of population, than any other country on the planet. Research results say she will be an excellent ambassador for Teatime biscuits.

The problem, once again, is, we're not sure she'll do the television and radio commercials (no one has asked her) or whether we can afford such a well-known ambassador. But the Lintas Auckland teams are risk-takers and doers. So, I head toward the phone.

After finding her number, I place a long distance call to England. I avoid her agent because I don't want to pay a substantial agent fee. Introductions are made. The market is explained, as well as the task. Then, we quickly babble about money. The answer is swift. "Yes of course. I love New Zealand."

Pam Ayres

Ayres is on a plane and in the film studio in days and the campaign is launched. Her financial needs are minimal. She is a joy to work with and is nicer in real life than the wonder lady we laugh along with on TV, or while listening to her comic releases. A consummate pro, she realizes the value of meeting Aulsebrooks management, the company team and the stockists. We are amazed, watching her *multi-task* responsibilities before it becomes common practice for all celebrities wanting to do it right.

One thing that is different this time, and why I believe Murphy is changing his style, is that we're winging it, without a lot of thought. This is dangerous. Risk is now becoming disproportionately high and we downplay careful reason and thought.

"SHE'LL BE RIGHT, MATE!"

New business wins continue without interruption despite our anger and increasingly wayward style.

A New Zealand brewer, Leopard of Hasting, needs a little help. The Australian beer brands, particularly the light lagers, are about to invade the vulnerable Kiwi market of beer swillers, or so we are told! With this in mind, a presentation is prepared for one of New Zealand's biggest brewers. With dash and dare we drive to the other side of the North Island, to the coastal city of Hastings, where it is located.

Three critical, but unexpected, marketing concepts are in the presentation. This time the team is well oiled: we're not winging it and it plays like a finely tuned orchestra. Think big, deliver the unexpected and don't worry about the detail that will be sorted later.

Within a few hours we make the necessary impact to get their interest. They stop talking and remain Stonehenge-quiet. The air is dead.

The first proposal is to create a brand-spanking new light lager, to combat a possible attack by Aussie light lagers. The name suggested is PAW lager, in a simple blue can with a large leopard paw print wrapped around the can! When ordering at a bar we suggest customers just growl - Grrrrrrr and a "PAW" will be delivered. That is the concept.

Easy we say, not having a clue about the challenge brewers' face. That is their job. But it's what excites prospective client: an entirely new product that has to be brewed and created by their team. It's challenging, but surprisingly, they believe, *"They can do it!"*

Buried within a number of other recommendations is the big one. We suggest they hire Richard Hadlee, New Zealand's greatest cricketer, as the spokesman for PAW and their export products. Yes, Richard Hadlee, the world's greatest cricketer, at the time, and a Kiwi.

The reason is simple. He has enormous international appeal and will help market their export products sold in England and worldwide. Leopard has a brand called New Zealand Export Lager Beer. Hadlee will be the lightning rod to attract international electricity. We show them a photo of Hadlee holding a can of beer, photographed on a cricket field in England. The headline, we suggest, would simply state, *"The world drinks our Export."* The ad is signed by Hadlee. It's a slam dunk as far as we're concerned.

Richard Hadlee

Sir Richard Hadlee, the thirty-year old Christchurch, New Zealand kid with the nickname "Paddles," because of his big feet, is on his way to worldwide fame and glory. Now he's to be the spokesman for one of New Zealand's most successful brewing companies.

The third critical point made is that we can begin work "the next day" and will get back to them with the initial steps a week later.

They remain dead quiet, but smiles are etched on their stony faces. As we leave, we sense a fuse has been lit in the darkened boardroom. But no one wants to be the first to react; they are frightened, but challenged.

We drive home to Auckland, quiet but elated. By now, the Auckland office, in my mind at least, has gained worldwide stature. We don't have the business yet, but we believe it's in the bag.

The next day, the phone rings and we're signed on. It's another victory and another highly visible account with worldwide possibilities for the Lintas billion-dollar network. Management Campaign Corner reported the coup on page 108 of the September 1981 issue.

The interesting fact is that Hadlee doesn't know a thing about our presentation.

The next steps are familiar from previous pages. I have to reach Hadlee and get him on board FAST. Leopard has to start brewing trials for PAW lager to be sure it can brew a light lager that will remain tasty when refrigerated. After all, Leopard has the serious problems of production: putting the lager in cans and distributing it throughout the country and beyond. A massive challenge, but inspiring when we see the results that can be achieved when people are motivated.

Success follows, as within a week Hadlee says, "Yes, mate."

Tracking down Paddles, we find him playing cricket in England. A crew from Westside Studios in London is dispatched to photograph him inside and outside, on field and off field. In the meantime, we've sent cans of lager and beer to use as props, until we can "strip-in" the new PAW labels that are being finalized.

What a success. What a hit. We have a spokesman to use in New Zealand and around the world. Sir Richard is ours, and is absolutely the right choice for the brewery.

The southern star shone brighter than ever that night, positioned right over 100 Greys Avenue in Auckland.

But once again, head office and the international network pay no homage to this outpost. Our success is ignored by Paris, London, New York and the kangaroo states. A simple telex of congratulations is all that is required. After all, this is a big international brand and probably the last chance for Lintas to save itself from disaster.

Pop stars get it, famous people get it, and great actors get it in the early stages of their careers. Self-importance and self-esteem puff up your sails and sweep you along to a point where you don't recognize yourself. It is dangerous. Egos, massive egos, emerge that will drive you up or push you down.

But to the outside world the puffed-up superstars from New Zealand drive along unnoticed. For the first time, I believe we can do it on our own. We do not need an international name on the door.

Chapter 6

COMING TOGETHER

After working eighteen years with multinationals in London, Brussels and West Africa, I've learned how they should operate. Reporting systems must be in place to keep head office informed, whether it's about day to day activity, new campaigns, innovative strategies, or new business gained. Many, including Lintas, send bulletins around the world to inform worldwide offices of business gains but I wasn't aware of many other means of communication. Newsletters should not be an excuse to avoid personal contact.

Senior people should know each other by their first names. There must be constant communication between the principals, if for no other reason than to ease temporary strain. An annual meeting between principals is a must. To its credit, Lintas, or perhaps the bosses at Interpublic, did hold such meetings, allowing Murphy to become familiar with other world leaders.

But other than the annual rah rah sessions, nothing else seemed to happen, whether because of lack of interest or because of Murphy's style. Very little is known about key players in other markets, including nearby Australia. In my view, they concluded our office was too small to really care about. Australians, in our nearby office, don't believe anything of significance happens in New Zealand, other than football. Hence, there is little familiarity. I am not aware of the name Bruce Harris until much later.

One evening, we celebrate at a restaurant in downtown Auckland, a classy, expensive restaurant for the well heeled.

The usual outgoing, fun-to-be-with Murf is distracted, maybe sulking, and it's obvious something troubles him. We talk, and dance around issues. He questions his future and mine. Talk turns to whether I'll remain in New Zealand, whether my wife is happy, whether the children are happy. There is no response from me, because I don't have an answer. The long gaps in conversation indicate Murphy is looking for a response to questions he is unwilling to ask directly. But if I think for a minute, I know he's fed-up with the leaderless generation at Lintas and is disappointed that his career has four flat tires: it's over. He wants to talk, but is finding it difficult to spark a dialogue.

Murphy has surrounded himself with a superb team and it's fair to say most in the agency adore his leadership style and remain loyal, unlike any relationship I've experienced before. Lintas Auckland is a love-in and we should all have been smoking pot, but we're not. There are no troublemakers in the agency; no one is backstabbing his leadership, even though in some quarters his reputation indicates he's an unpredictable, rebellious, hard drinking, son-of-a-bitch. But that's not the feeling with staff at other agency branches.

The Wellington office that reports to Murphy seems to be a giant marshmallow; soggy, rudderless and uninspired, with bits of back-stabbing spreading in a circle centered around a few. My contact with the Wellington office suggests Michael is probably envious of David's success. He's certainly not the kind of guy who will say anything complimentary about the hard-driving, egotistical Murphy.

As the wine flows, the office team is discussed and we agree the agency needs another account director, as business is still growing rapidly.

David Downham

David Downham, the commercial manager, secretary, financial guy and whatever he is required to be, is a critical member of the team. Murphy needs leadership in the financial area and the quiet, articulate Downham provides it. We like him, we trust him and he's funny. The taciturn Downham is also the mouthpiece to Sydney, as he reports regularly to Bruce Marsden, the Sydney financial director on money matters. They have a good rapport and like each other. So we agree Downham is a fabulous asset, and remember what Henry VI said, *"In thy face I see the map of honour, truth and loyalty."*

Mike Howard

Mike Howard, or "Howdo," as we call him, is media director. Gregarious, good-looking, with a mop of sandy hair, he is all smile and twinkly blue eyes, an outdoor type who will go out of his way to avoid trouble. Young Howdo is everyone's friend; he's a ton of Kiwi with a big heart, and first to invite us to a Kiwi barby. "Just throw anything on the open fire, roast 'er up, slam down a couple of brewskies and you're at the altar of Sunday leisure," he'd say. Not only is he a great guy, he knows the media, knows how to plan and knows how to buy television, radio, newspaper, outdoor and all the rest of the shit on the menu. He'd say something like, "Advertising is 85% confusion, 15% commission." I think he borrowed that from American media guru Joseph Levine.

Howdo is a good cobber, a keeper for sure.

We also talk about *Tim Roberts*. Everyone likes Roberts, especially the clients. Black scruffy hair, blue eyes and a square face. Roberts is a rock-solid, middle class, sports-nut who most in this region love to wag to about what's going on. Roberts, too, opens the front door for the usual Sunday barby, but Roberts adds a little more wine to the celebration, making it iffy to drive home. He's a keeper, not just because we like him, but also because clients trust him and he gets things done. He delivers the goods.

Tim Roberts

David Russell

The other member of the in-team is *David Russell*, our production manager. The same assets are evident: neat guy, lovely family, hard working and has a hard focus on bottom line results. Russell is one of the few who never makes a production "bluey". As anyone in the business will tell you, one or two errors in production and you write off hundreds of thousands of dollars in lost revenue. Russell doesn't make mistakes. The Russells, too, are a sociable lot who open their doors to us for many a long afternoon or evening of fun. They, too, have the ideal family: two children, just like most of the team.

The final member of the inner core has not joined the agency yet, but will be indispensable because of expanding business. We have yet to interview him, but we know he has to be a local hire.

After a long afternoon at Napoleon's, Murphy's feeling better, almost as if he's decided something and is putting together a team. I for one don't know what he is up to, but if forced to question him, I'd say, *"When are you leaving and are you setting up your own agency, with these guys?"* But I don't.

If anything frightens me, it's the thought I might be stranded in New Zealand without a job, trying to bring up a young family. Which begs the question whether the Lintas senior staff is going to be wiped out in Auckland. Now is not the time to scare my wife, but I know she is hearing things from other wives that frighten her at our barbys. Indeed, many speculate that something big is about to blow, but I push the thought back in the bottle.

As I think about our relationship with Lintas when we leave the restaurant, I can recall having only one meeting with Lintas global

management, when someone from Paris dropped by for a roll in the hay. I've not spoken to anyone in Sydney or know a name; it's like they're on *Pink Floyd's Dark Side of the Moon*.

Driving home, I drop by BP and, much to my surprise, I'm given King Smurf, the Smurf of all Smurfs, as a thank you for buying gas. I ask Karen, the manager, if I can have another King. The Kiwis are a lovely lot. *"Yea mate, of course,"* she replies. My spirits are lifted as I head home to family.

When I arrive, the children are in bed, so I take the King Smurfs to their bedrooms and tuck them under their pillows.

Beverley, too, has a surprise when I return downstairs. She grabs my hand and we tiptoe to the wicker chair to be introduced to seven beautiful little Burmese kittens. I stroke them gently, starting up their purr motors, and feel the uncertainty of everything discussed with Murphy drift away.

In the morning, I'm told many of the teachers at school have told the children they must head north to visit Waitangi and the Bay of

Islands. After all, treaty house is there and it's the birthplace of the nation of New Zealand. We decide the trip will be something to look forward to in the warmer months, when the kittens are sold and we can leave our two breeding cats in a cat hotel.

Giving birth at Boodles

It's the middle of August, the darkest of the winter months, and Murphy wants to talk; maybe to wrap up what we started a few days back. By now, he's settled and has returned to the Murphy of old. The signals are there: he's combed his black hair and his moustache is turned up at both ends, which gives the appearance of a bigger than usual smile.

What I didn't know at the time is that this lunch will be an end and a beginning. Nor did I speculate that years later I will devote part of a book to this historic lunch at Boodles.

Boodles is a tiny '80s hip restaurant, near the corner of Remuera Road and Victoria Avenue, just next to the post office. The exterior of Boodles is a wedding cake treasure, with a washed yellow façade. It's all fashion, candle light and beautiful people enjoying noisy conversation. This is where the trendy crowd go to be seen, made more enjoyable this evening by a Canadian singing duo of wayward Vancouverites: a cross between Gordon Lightfoot and Ian and Sylvia.

The restaurant is a perfect setting for the most beautiful society to meet to celebrate. And it's in Remuera, God's gift to privileged Kiwis on their way to becoming kings and queens. The community is known for the privilege afforded the citizenry's children, like King's College. The aroma of French breads from the Baguette across the street teases the nose. Marcel, with a toothy smile, is the owner and he bakes the most beautiful breads this side of Paris.

So Boodles is familiar in Remuera, even to me. And here the picaroons meet: Murphy and Truman facing each other, one washed and happy, the other suspicious. Murphy starts by waltzing around issues as if on the dance floor. After a few months building the agency, it's obvious we've developed a special bond that makes us much stronger *as a team* than separately. Large clients, including brewers, producers of packaged goods and hard goods and the tourism business have rushed into the agency, and we've created successful campaigns that moved sales beyond expectation. We have exploded as a team. Murphy believes the objectives he is trying to reach have been surpassed in spades.

I explain that the company has been terrific to me and I have no doubt they'll honour whatever requests I make, including requesting a posting to Sydney, Australia where I've always longed to settle.

We're enjoying a raucous dinner, celebrating the good life and our achievements to date. Then, he begins to discuss an idea he's been thinking about for a while. I could sense it coming by his excited shuffle: shifting his arm and leg positions, opening his big hands, fingers outstretched and that engaging grin, the wide-screen smile. Yes, he is ready to talk. And this is the way I remember it.

First, he wants me to understand that he's been loyal for more than ten years and has successfully worked his way up the corporate ladder to manage the New Zealand operation. Because I have been working so closely with him, he knows I discovered he's a complex sort of man when it comes to marketing strategies. Murphy babbles on about his life and reminds me he's a Brit with Irish lineage: an ex-Constable, and able to speak on his feet. We laugh about how clients leap to their feet with excitement when Murphy gushes about an idea or a strategy. He's as tall as summer wheat and usually has a twinkle in his eyes and a winning smile, crowned by that thick bushy moustache. He has the ingredients to be a great leader and is a talented marketing and advertising man. What else is there to say?

He knows clients like and respect him and the successful team he's put together. I remind him staff and clients know it's an agency with a memorable and charismatic leader. Sure, he can drink anyone under the table, keep them laughing for hours on end and keep the restaurant rocking till six in the morning. He'll take clients to a strip joint if that's what a client wants. In so many ways, he is a model for all account-servicing people to follow. In other ways, his life is wholly experimental.

The real reason for the idea Murphy seems eager to talk about is clearly based on his frustration with Lintas. He simply confirms everything he's said, repeatedly: they ignore us; we don't get recognition for our achievements and certainly Lintas doesn't have a plan for his future. His final request is for better compensation than he's garnered for the past few years. No detail is discussed. It's not the words that are uttered, nor the wayward points, but the severity of the tone, his flailing arms and the depth of passion in his voice. A few issues have grown into a monster that speaks volumes about his present state of mind and what he's about to say out loud!

I HAVE AN IDEA

It starts quite matter of factly.

"I have an idea," says Murphy, to which I reply, "What's that?"

With a slurp of wine, the plan is ready to lay on the table.

By now, we're both nervously ordering additional glasses of Chablis to settle our nerves or to use as an excuse should the plot get too thick – we can always *"blame the demon drink"* we think, or *"deny it all."*

"I resign," suggested Murphy. *"You follow me, and we set up our own agency!"* That is the gist of the proposal that I remember.

He is passionate about the decision. He's had enough. His energies are about to be directed toward forming his own agency and sailing on alone, or with a partner.

His eyes sparkle, that cinemascope smile appears again. Then, there's a long pause. The plan is simple, he says. We'll just set up on our own and try to attract new accounts. But we'll not solicit Lintas business. Oh, no. If Lintas accounts want to join later, that's their prerogative in a free society. "What of the staff?" I ask. David's answer is simple and daring, with words to the effect that, "I think we know who we'd like, so they might follow us a few months later."

"Well, what do you think? I'd like your support," says Murphy. I pause; think about the difficulties I will have after arriving in New Zealand just eight months earlier. *"What will be left of the Auckland office with Murphy gone? I'd be unemployed; I'd be on the street in no time. Will my work permit still be valid if I leave Lintas?"* I ponder.

The next few seconds will shape both of our futures for years to come. It's an awkward exchange, as I remember, with both of us feeling uncomfortable. What if I decide to call Lintas and tell them Murphy is planning to quit? Is David setting me up to see if he can blame me for turning him against Lintas? Yes, this is a test of my loyalty to the office, or maybe just to Murphy. As Beverley and Anita Murphy are already fast friends, I know Anita must be aware of what he is saying. *"Hell, our young daughters Michelle and Nicole are friends with their children Matthew and Amanda. The families are so close spiritually,"* I thought.

I'm scrambling for words. Murphy isn't sure of the outcome and will not know what the result will be, as most staff and clients will not follow anyway: they'll probably wait for a new managing director to be appointed by Lintas. Without thinking, I stupidly reason Lintas might just roll over and say, *"Oh well, we lost Murphy, so the Auckland office will be merged with the Wellington office."* Naïve, but a possibility!

One factor that I cannot ignore is the arrival a few weeks back of a senior member of the agency, here to look at the books, have discussions about accounts and give us the usual rah-rah party. He turned me against them that weekend. I never forgave Lintas for this shameful act, but it did confirm Murphy's musings that they didn't care about business or improving the skills of the employees. We were simply cogs in a massive billion-dollar money machine: merely numbers; little bits that could be replaced if targets are not met.

The man's actions left me shaking, believing they really didn't give a damn about New Zealand no matter how dedicated and loyal we are. The decision to turn tail on Lintas happened in minutes: it is a turning point.

A FATEFUL DECISION

I'm not sure of the exact wording, but my reply is something like, "Yes, I'm in, but I have to think about it and discuss it with my wife first, as this decision will be monumental and historic."

That lunch leads to the birth of the Murphy Truman agency: Boodles bistro in Remuera, the same place where Sir Edmund Hillary has been spotted.

An hour later, what we agreed to is like a slap in the face as we step into the crisp winter air, feet pointed in different directions. I probably took it all in, fully prepared to give it serious thought because I suspected he is going to resign, but didn't expect him to really set up on his own. I also sense that without my support, he might not resign from Lintas and this story will never have begun.

The dangers of course are perilous if the new venture fails, we'll be bankrupt rather quickly, with no way to pay food bills and rent. I certainly couldn't afford the move back to Canada.

In the midst of this dilemma, we're invited to take a business trip to the South Pacific island of Samoa to make a new business presentation and the agency is working flat out.

Terry Hall has produced fabulous images for our new campaign for Paradise Airlines. Murphy and I are smiling, because we know it'll probably be another win.

The next day, we begin interviews for another account director.

A pleasant fellow from Newson Lodge in Auckland applies for the position and wins hands down. He's another with experience and that lovely soft Kiwi touch that clients like. Murphy and I welcome the newest member to the team.

Knowing that we'll probably resign shortly makes this decision very questionable, but we do hire the suave intellectual with solid family ties.

Jon Muir joins Lintas and becomes account director on many of the new accounts, including Aulsebrooks, and is another leader with a tick beside his name.

Jon Muir

Chapter 7

A FINAL STUPID ACT

TO PARTY – WITHOUT REASON

It's early September, 1981. The party went on and on, interrupted by sick staff members relieving themselves through the haze of cigarette smoke in the boardroom.

A phone call earlier in the day has sent our hearts racing. The pitch team raced to the off-license in search of wine, beer, spirits and tropical grub to celebrate winning the Paradise Airlines business.

It's an opportunity to promote a South Pacific airline while earning even more revenue for the agency. What a win! Free travel to paradise is promised whenever we wish. And being pampered by the most beautiful sky hostesses in the South Pacific archipelago is another big bonus. We're awash in dreams. After all, the Western Samoan islands, home for Samoans for at least two thousand years, are filled with history, romance and legend. From the early days of kings and queens to the arrival of the pakeha (Europeans) and missionaries, Western Samoa is more than magic; it's a heavenly paradise.

Special islands of extraordinary beauty, where turquoise lagoons lap onto unspoiled white beaches lined with coconut palms, the islands have an abundance of cascading waterfalls, rich green rainforests and mist-enshrouded mountain peaks, all contained within a sparkling necklace of coral reefs.

We keep repeating, "On with the party, the big dream will follow."

The walls of the boardroom are covered with the advertising images that have won us the business: beautiful people, beautiful planes, soon to be painted in tropical colors, each and every one a different lush colour, aircraft tails festooned with different birds of paradise. Two weeks of research, discovery and imagination paid off.

We draw pictures of beautiful stewardesses, gift wrapped in crisply pressed skirts, in keeping with Samoan tradition. As soon as you board a Paradise Islands 737 airliner, the traditional umu or Samoan barbecue will dance in travelers' heads. Passengers will be served fresh tropical fruits, accompanied by wondrous coconut drinks, Samoa's most popular.

The ads on the walls say it all. *"Picture tropical gardens of majestic coconut palms, bougainvilleas, scented frangipanis and orchids."*

The campaign theme is, *"Paradise Airlines. BIRDS OF PARADISE."* According to Dan Nuttley, representing the client, it's a winner. The world is awaiting such a discovery and we have the keys to the fantasy.

As the party progresses, drinks fan the flames of our imagination. The irony is that not a soul on the pitch team, nor any of the agency staff, has been on the airline or traveled to Samoa. This is a campaign ignited by innocence, imagination and unbridled dreams. The celebration will soon be the irony that switches the hot engine off. We've leapt a little too quickly at an alcohol-induced passion for life in paradise, that will continue into the late hours, as the crescendo of rhythmic sound mingles with the tinkle of ice cubes on the tongue until early morning.

The next day, the truth began to sink in. We have been *short-listed* only, just short-listed, but we've been told by Nuttley that we're guaranteed to win the business.

Just three days later, we'll repeat the presentation in Samoa with government officials. It's merely a rubber stamp, said the Australian recruited to find an advertising agency for Paradise Airlines. He's seen what we created and fell off his chair with excitement. Nuttley's nickname in the islands is *Tusitala*. What it means is unraveled much later in Western Samoa.

A Hint from "Tusitala"

Nuttley tells us he'll not be present at the final presentation to the ministers in Samoa. Mr. Assi Halle will meet us when we arrive. Halle is referred to as the Minister of *Nothing*.

Paradise Airlines will fly us from Auckland in one of their new Boeing 737 aircraft. David Murphy and I will make the presentation, just as we did in Auckland.

The Aggie Grey Hotel is where we will stay for two nights, at government expense. This is also where the presentation will take place.

Anyone who has done this before knows the first presentation is usually great, doing it a second time is often better, but doing it a third or fourth time chews up your enthusiasm and impromptu ad-libbing ruins the show. As this is our second shot, it should be terrific.

What we don't know is who'll be in the audience, other than Assi Halle, which when said quickly has a nasty connotation in English. There will be fourteen ministers, the one to impress being the Minister of Everything, who is very close to the Prime Minister. They'll all be wearing white lava-lavas (sarong-like garments I refer to as dresses) that always give me the titters.

Because Samoan democracy is based on the British parliamentary system, shaken a bit, to take Samoan custom into account, we're relaxed about the fairness of the process.

The night before departure, David and I agree Western Samoa is an emerging tourism destination with few parallels in the world. The gentle climate blesses these islands with a bounty of natural beauty. Brochures show magnificent white and black sandy beaches, rugged mountains, steep gorges, many waterfalls, lava fields, blowholes, dormant volcanoes (last erupted in 1911), fantastic tropical vegetation and exotic flowers. Aside from the jewel-box of natural wonders, the Samoans are, reputedly, generous people.

Western Samoa is regarded as the cradle of Polynesia. It is believed the islands contain Hawaiki, the place from which the original Polynesians, guided by the stars, voyaged to other Pacific Islands over 2,000 years ago. Hell, Robert Louis Stevenson, one of my favourite authors, said it is paradise on earth. He is buried here, according to his last request. How can it not be a special place? I ask as I slowly "cark out" for the day.

A WAKE-UP CALL

Morning in Auckland is the well-reported heaven on earth. The scattered cloud cover is high, with wide swashes of orange and vermillion hiding in the morning light. Throw in a rainbow arched over the harbor and a hint of morning mist and you have a beautiful Turner sky and seascape.

After our taxi drops us at Auckland International airport, the tiny 737 sucks us through the front cabin door. A woman with a moustache, one long hair growing from her chin and a surly manner, abruptly seats us. *"Hmmmmmph,"* we think. This isn't the doorway to paradise. A glance around the cabin reveals a stark interior and a half-full cabin. Sina, as the tiny 737 is dubbed, rips into Turner's painting with lightheaded abandon, as if Sina doesn't want to go home. We're on our way to paradise?

Within an hour or two, carrots, peas, mashed potatoes and a tough steak are dumped on our eating shelf by the moustache, as she's having a bad hair day. Hell, we thought, pigs get a better reception in the morning.

The images we created start to peel away as Sina bumps its way around a black typhoon. The captain stumbles through the cabin on his way to the rear toilet. He keeps pulling up his pants, as they're falling to the ground. He's a bit messy. Trousers are wrinkled and the backside is polished to a high shine because he's spent his life sitting on something hard. His tie is crooked and his stare uneven. This doesn't create the sense of confidence one expects from a captain of Paradise Airlines. The illusion is crumbling at a rapid rate.

But nothing quite matches the chat I have with someone familiar with the airline who is travelling as a passenger on the return flight to Apia. Without prompting, he regales me with stories of the airline over the past few months. This disgruntled employee has no idea who the travelers are.

First, he says, the aircraft has been decertified because employees have stripped the craft of its safety gear. And it doesn't matter if it's replaced, someone else will remove the stuff again. Life raft, flashlights, axes, fire extinguishers and food reserves for survivors in a raft, the list went on, are all gone. Plus, I'm told the quality of flight service is ranked below zero. The stewardess on board that day was feeding chickens a month ago. One pilot who flew internally within the islands of Western Samoa has glasses as thick as the bottoms of Coke bottles. He has so much trouble seeing, he relies on the co-pilot's eyes when landing. By the time we reach Apia, it's apparent we're on the wrong plane or this trip is the original flight to hell. We're told this is a typical flight on PA's only jet aircraft.

The pilot lands on one wheel with a thump, then rolls down the washboard runway with a shudder, gumpf, bang, thump, rattle; hits a rabbit, phewwwww and slides on mud to a final stop in "paradise."

THE SPY MUSEUM OF THE SOUTH PACIFIC

Motoring from the airport is another disappointing experience: nothing, absolutely nothing lives up to the words we've written to describe this pearl in the Pacific. Assi Halle didn't show up to greet us.

Rusted car bodies lay on dirty beaches, uncared for fales (homes) line the route, streets are badly signposted, bridges are ready to collapse, and undisciplined gardens lay about. The list went on as the dream is shattered into billions of pieces of shit. The first cry of sanity is me screaming something like, *"I'm seeing things. Let's get out of here. This is a bloody bad dream!"*

After unpacking, we flee in different directions in search of paradise. I'm determined to get to the top of Mount Vaba to ogle the Pacific from on high.

With the assistance of a guide, I trek up Mount Vaba, where Robert Louis Stevenson is buried. Maybe he saw something from on high that'll get my heart racing again. The walk up the mountain is difficult, but stimulating. The scenery along the way is lush and tropical, just as Stevenson promised. Who can forget Ben Gunn or Long John Silver of *Treasure Island* fame? If Stevenson liked the place, maybe we're being unfair.

Once I conquer Mount Vaba, I look about. It's true, the view is spectacular, no matter which way you gaze. An octagonal table sits to one side, where visitors rest and eat while paying silent tribute to Stevenson. A thatch style roof is constructed over the table to protect visitors from the rain. The high ground where the tomb rests, is surrounded by tiny pink flowers, providing the best view of the sweeping Pacific. Stevenson obviously sat here a century ago and loved the spectacle.

The grave of Robert Louis Stevenson

A plaque on his tomb says something I recall about Dan Nuttley, the guy who selected us as a short-listed agency in the review. The plaque said, *"This is the road of loving hearts, hewn by the people of Samoa for Tusitala – Robert Louis Stevenson."* Aha, I think, Stevenson is called Tusitala and so is Dan Nuttley, perhaps there is a link. First, I'll have to find out what it means in English.

The truth is revealed later when a waiter at the hotel says it means "storyteller." This means Dan Nuttley is either a storyteller or a *bullshitter*. No one can enlighten us for certain, but the latter seems to describe him well at this juncture.

A poem on the tomb, written by Robert Louis Stevenson, reveals a little more about his thoughts. *"Under the wide and starry sky, dig the grave and let me die. Glad did I live and gladly die, and I laid me down with a will. This is the verse you gave for me: Here he lies where he longed to be: Home is the sailor, home from the sea, and the hunter home from the hill."*

I'm alone with Robert Louis Stevenson that day, as no one else has ventured up to say hello. It touches me deeply knowing we all are so alone in death.

That evening, the pitch team rehearses again. Then we meet in the bar, with Assi Halle, the Minister or Nothing, and a number of local groupies.

The bar at Aggie Grey's is famous for many things. It's the hangout for government workers and chiefs, and it's the rendezvous for the world's broken-down spies (so I'm told). The CIA, Mi6, the Russians, the Chinese, the Aussies and the Canadians are here, tracking the movement of subs and naval ships throughout the vast Pacific because Samoa is in an ideal location. As this is the era before satellites, they use old-fashioned technology to watch each other. Binoculars, Pentax cameras with long lenses, mirrors and looking through the bottom of beer mugs: they're all at it in their fuzzy years.

These guys and a woman have a few things in common. They're wrinklies, wear sunglasses, speak in hushed tones, move with difficulty and flash the talas (the local currency) or U.S. bucks, with impunity. By the end of the evening, they're always streeted (drunk). The only name I recall is Ethel, known as Lala by her fellow spies. She can shag 'em, bag 'em, or gag 'em with the best, according to Gorgi, the Russian spy. It appears most spies are put out to pasture at Aggie Grey's rather than undertaking real spy duties. They're like the Dad's Army of the South Pacific. This lifestyle is part of their retirement package, play-acting at being hot and in control, when in fact they're '50s *has-beens* from central casting, doing a show for the tourists, who never show up.

The evening ends with a fire-dancing extravaganza by twelve muscular waiters from the hotel. While watching, we scoff things like sea cucumbers and sea urchins, bananas cooked in coconut milk and taro leaves with dollops of coconut cream on top. Breadfruit is also served, cooked in coconut milk, along with papaya also cooked in: you guessed it! Coconut dishes abound. Why not: we discovered the basis of Samoan cuisine is coconut milk.

The next morning we will make our presentation: it'll be a long and difficult day. The show will start at 10 A.M. in the same enormous bar where we celebrated the previous evening. Sixteen people will sit through the presentation. That is democracy, Samoan style. Dan Nuttley says it's just a formality. We've won the account, even thought *technically* we're only on a short list. Which, technically, means other competing agencies will present for the business. How many? When? We've not been told.

ILLUSIONS ARE ILLUSORY

Assi Halle, the Minister of dick-all meets with us at 9 A.M. to confirm the meeting at 10 A.M. Yes, he confirms they'll be here for the slide show by 10 or so. In the meantime, we set up our charts, screen and the advertising campaign ideas created by Terry Hall and his team. Assi Halle asks if anyone can speak Samoan, as some of the attendees do not speak English well and Samoan is a second language for the people, along with Chinese-Samoan. We are advised that members from the HRPP, SNDP, SPCP, SAAP, the SLP and others will be in attendance. But the only person who really matters is the Minister of Everything. Not a clue what this means, other than pandemonium. Yes, it'll be a dumb presentation for sure.

In a flash, an audience starts to appear. We don't know who they are, as they're not introduced. By now, we don't know what we're supposed to say, or what they want to hear. Would anything make sense to this group? Why are we presenting to the entire government of the people, and the opposition, in an open bar at Aggie Grey's Hotel? It's supposed to be a rubber-stamp meeting with a few insiders to show them how we're proposing to lift tourism and the image of Paradise Airlines.

Around 10 A.M., cats wander into the staging area, followed by a few dogs, two parrots, an assortment of police officers, a spy we recognize from the previous night and, finally, a government official. The spy falls asleep before we begin the presentation. The first official person precisely chooses his sitting spot. He is followed by a rather large human wearing a skirt. He quickly orders a beer. By 10:30, the last official people parade down the hallway into the bar and sit on a bank of stools. There they are, a motley crew of men in skirts awaiting the arrival of the Minister of Everything and maybe the Prime Minister. They give signals to each other, mumble politely, start tapping their fingers impatiently and ask us to wait for one last person. This, we presume, will be the Prime Minister.

Ten minutes later, the Minister of Everything gives us a signal by banging a stick on the wooden floor. Just bangs the stick: no words, nothing; just an impatient look on his face as he thumps the wood as loudly as he can, probably to wake up the audience. About now, a Perry Como record starts to play in the bar. Someone has switched on the radio.

We're now facing the most hostile crowd we've ever entertained, some drinking beer, some with their eyes shut, a few snoring, a menagerie of cats, dogs and parrots rushing around looking for food and a dog defecating on the carpet. The bar area is filled with the melodies of Perry Como. But, no Prime Minister. The show must go on, so we proceed, without a script.

You've Got Ten Minutes, Go!

Rule number one when presenting is: know your audience and work to gain their sympathy. Spot the key receiver of your message and make sure he gets the message loud and clear. Speak slowly and clearly, as most of these bozos don't want to be here, and probably can't understand English let alone Canadian or Kiwi versions of the language.

The script went out the window. The slide show went. So did the flip charts. Show them pretty pictures to get them excited. It's good old impromptu comedy, highly focused with lots of walking around in front of the audience. After all, we have to keep them awake. We have to make them understand what advertising is all about, and the benefits for their airline and tourism industry, because they don't know why we're here!

Forget Marketing 101. We now rely on English 101 as a starting point. Hell, half these guys don't even know they have an airline funded by the government. Some ask why we would use their money to promote travel to Samoa or advertise in a foreign country like Australia or New Zealand. A few asked what kind of paint we're proposing to use. Some said they could buy paint cheaper in their own store. Paint? What the hell are they talking about; paint? Another asks about wood and laughs. Must be an inside joke. We didn't get it, none of it.

We missed the audience by a country mile, and they missed our message. Like busses in a thick London fog, we passed each other in the bar. Within thirty minutes most leave, following the departure of the Minister of Everything in his bright red dress.

In summary, they don't know what we're talking about and they don't know why we're here. They believe we sell paint, some kind of paint.

To this day I don't understand what we were doing in paradise. What were we supposed to paint? Perhaps the aircraft, maybe the hotel, possibly the main street of Apia, or their fales? Maybe we got it all wrong and our Australian friend didn't understand them at all. He just did a job, made a recommendation, received his royalty payment and fled. We agree on one thing: Nuttley should be strung up. Tusitala earned his nickname of *bullshitter* honestly.

UPON REFLECTION!

That evening, we partied alone at Aggie Grey's, celebrating the fact that we've been duped. And it has cost thousands of dollars for the Samoan treasury to fly us here.

We did reflect on the poor devils that live in this difficult country, living through what I thought is poverty and sacrifice. Walking the streets later, we see the good in people. There is beauty in their warm smiles as the setting sun paints everything in golden light.

As for clients, we never heard from Dan Nuttley. He did his job, got his commission and moved on to another misadventure.

The islands survive, governments change in a democracy, the Prime Minister is shuffled every five years, the airline keeps flying AND, without doubt, some visitors still think it's paradise.

Our eye was off the ball; that's why we were suckered into pitching the Paradise Airline account.

Our thoughts are clearly on other matters. Within hours, carried along by the momentum of our failed adventure in paradise, we had the most difficult decision to make.

On the way home from Auckland Airport, I directed the taxi driver to BP. Wow. This time, I put Grumpy Smurf in my pocket, which said it all. I come to believe every time I buy gasoline a message is passed along from my little blue friends.

Chapter 8

HEY, WE JUST QUIT!

We're tired but energized; Murphy's face says he's had enough.

Support, encouragement, recognition are not forthcoming. We'll move on.

Some think Murphy is a dreamer, maybe even a puffed-up egotistical pommy with ambitions beyond his abilities. Many, who walk down similar hallways, with doors slammed on all sides, know the feeling of abandonment. For him, it's over.

After a lot of discussion with my wife and after sitting down with the children and just talking, the decision is made to leave the firm and set up an agency as a partner with Murphy.

My reason is simple. Lintas Auckland will collapse without Murphy's leadership. A new person will not be able to duplicate his dynamic qualities. Lintas will lose clients without Murphy's marketing input. In my mind, there's only one solution to the dilemma: follow the leader.

I don't think Lintas will stand with me if I stay. I believe they'll abandon me because I'm a "Murphy-man." A new leader will ease me out and replace me with a person he selects. There are many instances of a leader being installed, then removing staff in the conga line, rather quickly. No, I feel better knowing we have something special that we can market by ourselves. Together we're so much better than each operating alone. I don't think a lot of clients will follow us to our new agency. It's not possible, as most have ironclad contracts with Lintas. Certainly, the two big accounts, Feltex and Aulsebrooks do. One has a thirty-day severance agreement. The other has to give three months warning of termination.

It's all go, and time to look to the future on our own!

The company will be called Murphy Truman Advertising. Murphy will be the senior partner and own about 40.1%. I am the second partner and will own 25%. We'll leave room for an international partner at 24.9% and the rest we'll sell to four or five senior partners, if they wish to join. This is the plan, according to an affidavit dated September 24, 1981, written by David J. Murphy and introduced as evidence by Michael John Fitzgerald O'Sullivan in the High Court of New Zealand.

The green on our corporate livery is to celebrate Murphy's Irish heritage. Letterhead and critical stationery is designed in an evening of hectic activity.

A place to start our business is located on Anzac Avenue. Nothing special, just a little office space for the two of us until we have clients and become established. But it will take further negotiating to secure the place, as nothing is certain about our future business success.

The only money I can contribute is tied up in our old house in Canada, which I'll sell to raise my share of the capital. I promise to do that.

David and Anita negotiate a loan against their Rama Rama property, to set up the finances for the new company: a courageous move by exceptional people.

At this point, we're determined to just resign and head out on our own. We're confident we'll pick up business quickly and add staff as needed. There is no plan to run and take business from Lintas, let alone some of the staff.

Our next moves are made carefully to avoid walking into a lawsuit. Murphy is a director of the company and heads up the New Zealand operations of SSC&B Lintas but has no written agreement about his employment. I am a director, and have a written employment agreement with Lintas. We believe a standard thirty days notice will be acceptable, but expect that after the announcement they'll encourage us to leave immediately. So, we will. I don't seek legal advice, as I've resigned in the past with no difficulty. That's the way it's done in adland.

During the next few days, we walk and talk carefully. A date is chosen to tender our resignations. It is to be *Tuesday, September 22, 1981*.

Legal and bank negotiations are concluded and we finally agree on a short-term lease on the Anzac property, a run-down place where we'll hang our hat while we build the new agency.

The two of us meet with clients on a regular basis, usually once a month, if possible. The meetings and lunches carry on, as most of the clients are tried and true friends. Most are as close as family and trust is something we share in abundance. They share things about their bosses and companies and we share the odd joke about our international partners. It's so comfortable and makes these relationships strapping and unbreakable. Besides, they all like and admire David and his team's skills, well beyond the usual agency-client relationships that I've experienced.

But our departure is to be above board and clean. In the coming days, I sense a few clients are a little unsettled and believe something is up.

As September 22 approaches, it's clear to David and me that we'll need a good support team when our own agency finds its footing. So we begin talking to some of our senior people asking what they will do if we resign. The answer is consistent: they'll think about it and might wish to join up later. Nothing requires heavy breathing. They know David is unhappy. Some remain quiet and believe it's merely frustration and hotheaded bullshit. A few who will eventually become partners just smile and laugh, believing I will not resign as I'm on a transfer and wouldn't risk my family's security.

The thought of failure has already cast a shadow over events as we approach the day we'll announce our resignations. The senior team of five is informed of our plan a few days earlier, and is asked to think about joining us sometime in the future. At this point, we do not know how they will finally react. It's their decision, not ours. Only two of us are resigning officially. That's it!

Our departures are to be above reproach, with simple letters of resignation to be telexed to Sydney regional office on September 22. We will be gone the next day. The big fear is that a client or two will terminate their agreement with Lintas and join the new team. Some of the staff might also want to join us. We do not know what the reaction will be. The general staff do not know about our pending resignations, but rumblings have surfaced. The reaction to our resignations is unpredictable. On one hand, it's an optimistic beginning, but the overtones could be far worse than we can imagine. What if they all want to join, then we'll have a problem?

After our resignations many will know it's over. I always believed that "…foolish people without understanding have ears, but hear not; have eyes but see not." (Jeremiah 5:21). That's what we believe. It's too late, the wheels have turned direction, we're heading on a new course. The sun is setting on the last chapter.

In fairness to a few good people, our inner five, David, Jon, Tim, Mike and David know the date we'll be parting. It's up to them to decide what to do, as there is no guarantee of jobs or business with Murphy Truman. As for clients, well, that's their decision. I have never seen a client dictated to about where to take his business.

Chapter 9

BACK 265 DAYS TO CHAPTER 1

September 22, 1981 5 P.M.

As staff depart, they're swallowed by a brooding winter evening, heavy with uncertainty.

They resigned minutes earlier, in a fit of passion and exhilaration, mixed with a little foreboding. They're thinking about next steps.

Should they rush to the unemployment centers the next morning, just in case the new agency collapses before it starts? After all, the new agency has no accounts and probably limited funds to pay wages.

Andrea, Beth, Julie and Lindsey have abandoned secure careers. Most have spent considerable time with Lintas. Others, like Kevin, Graham, and Joanne head home to Grey Lynn, Glenfield and Parnell in a daze, to await phone calls telling them where to meet the next day. It's an uncertain time for staff.

With this move, regular pay cheques will stop. Most must pay rent, or mortgages and they'll need money to buy food.

Deep down, staffers like Julie Yonge and stalwart Andrea Gordon have resolute confidence in Murphy's passionate dream and this keeps them running till next morning.

Pretty little Nicole Smith, my producer, who joined recently from Wellington, is plainly frightened. Her lips are blue, her eyes are moist, her tiny body is shivering in the night air.

Later that evening, phone calls telling them where to meet the next day puff up their sails, indicating a good head wind and calmer seas ahead.

David and I, along with four senior members, (Timothy J. Roberts, Jon F. Muir, Michael Howard and David Russell) have resigned and will provide leadership. We have so much to do. We must keep running.

Chapter 10:

A NEW ERA DAWNS
A BATTLE BEGINS

DAVID VS. GOLIATH

The next day, September 23, 1981, staff and management meet at our temporary Anzac office in Takapuna City, near Lake Pupuke. "Lake Pukey" has connotations that reflect the mood of the time. It's an industrial warehouse, not what clients expect after the civility of Greys Avenue, but it's a temporary home for the three or four employees we thought might join us. We are wrong about the number.

Within hours we're told most of the clients also joined the exodus, indicating trouble ahead. It is a walkout on an unprecedented scale. The realization sets in that most of the staff and most of the clients wish to join us at our new agency.

Thirty days is the usual time for clients to fire and hire a new agency and in one instance a three month break is needed, but we still believe we need the files. Indications are that a number of major clients will simply fire Lintas, wait the thirty days, then award their business to the new agency.

A Letraset sign on a door states, "Murphy Truman Advertising – MTA Reception."

Surprise, surprise, nearly fifteen staffers squeeze into the tiny space, most working on the floor. The seniors, Julie, Andrea and Jill, scurry around the premises getting things in order. The phones are operational on the first day (as placed into evidence by Michael O'Sullivan) after O'Sullivan talked to Feltex.

Our new number, 778-920, rung off the hook not only with questions about the fallout from the walkout, but the usual bevy of suppliers wanting assurances their bills will be paid. Paying bills is the least of our worries. We have a mass payroll to meet, as well as the usual utility bills and we have no clients to provide immediate income.

Murphy Truman doesn't even have a typewriter, let alone a photocopier.

By now we know Lintas will respond. The resignations have supposedly been telexed to Sydney by David Downham, our mole working with the remaining three staff members left at Lintas Auckland. Downham informed Mike O'Sullivan, the head man in Wellington, then said he would call Bruce Harris in Sydney to inform him. It took three days for the information to reach Sydney.

The resignation the previous day of Timothy J. Roberts summed up the staff mood at the time. It said, *"Please accept my resignation effective 22nd September 1981. The resignation of David Murphy and Richard Truman has made my situation here (at Lintas) untenable."* That is the mood of everyone. The situation in Auckland, without leadership, will be impossible. The biggest career risk for employees would have been to stay, so they joined in the exodus.

That same day, September 23, I agree to buy 24,999 shares in the new company for $12,500. I will pay later, when I sell my house in Canada.

My company, Richard Truman Associates, consists of my wife Beverley and me. It is an arrangement I had made with Lintas Auckland to reduce our taxes. It is an agreement that Lintas appears unwilling to make with Murphy and is one of the reasons for the resignation.

Three days later, the news strikes Harris who is asked to put his warrior's armour on again.

Harris is the chosen one, about to do battle on behalf of the global operations. But why did it take three days for the resignations to get to Sydney? After all, Wellington headman Michael O'Sullivan *knew the next day* and was in Lintas' office in Auckland mid-day the next day, two days prior to Sydney being informed. Why hadn't O'Sullivan informed Sydney, or had he? Was he waiting until Downham informed them?

Goliath is slow off the mark

Three days later
Friday, September 25
SSC&B Lintas
157 Walker Street, North Sydney

One thousand, three hundred and forty miles across the Tasman, in Sydney, Australia, Bruce Harris is sitting quietly at his desk. Harris, started as a junior copywriter, worked his way through the ranks to creative director and then earned his keep as chairman and managing director of the Australian operation. The big man has clout and influence and is the right man to direct this battle.

Harris is relaxed, feet up, reading business reports. The week is nearly over and he's debating whether to have a Friday evening drink with a couple of the agency's executives before heading home to his wife Shirley and daughters, Jennifer, Vicki and the youngest, Merrilee.

Harris, as he's called by friends, is in his final year as CEO of Lintas Sydney. Englishman Roger Neill is being shown the ropes, as he'll be his replacement. Harris intends to bow out by the end of the year, just three months away.

Bruce Marsden, the financial director of the Sydney operation, and his assistant rush to see Harris, to alert him to what they soon call a conspiracy.

Marsden's equivalent in New Zealand, David Downham, has called to tell him of the walkout by the Auckland office: most of the staff and, possibly, some accounts. To make things worse, the breakaway team has launched an agency called Murphy Truman and is already operational. The seventeen resignations from staff members landed on Marsden's desk earlier that day, along with the resignations of Murphy and me.

Murphy's resignation simply stated, "I, David John Murphy, do hereby resign as a Director of the Company to take effect immediately upon receipt by you of this letter of resignation – (dated September 22, 1981). My resignation stated, "This is to inform you of my resignation, effective immediately." (dated September 23, 1981).

Why the three days delay by Downham in telling Marsden? The resignations are dated September 22/23, it is now September 25. Is this an intentional delay by our mole, Downham, who is still working with Lintas, to allow the new agency to get things rolling?

The news shocks fifty seven year old Harris, who is just beginning to relax and think about Christmas and a career change a few weeks away. Sparks fly: he grits his teeth. Harris worked hard to get to this level. *"Bad timing?"* he asks himself. He walks to the window, stares at the view of Sydney Harbor Bridge and North Sydney and then, with a steely gaze, determines he must act decisively.

Harris knows he must work fast, faster than Murphy, to knock the breakaway group off balance. But we have a three-day head start.

The Harris strategy is to spoil and retrieve: spoil the breakaway gang's efforts and retrieve as many of the accounts and staff as possible. From more than a thousand miles away, the task appears a little easier than the daunting project it'll become.

A council of war is held in Harris' office to determine next steps. The results are recorded by Harris's secretary Suzie and orders are issued with military precision.

First, Harris must track down the key man responsible for the region, Jean-Francois Lacour, who is doing business in India. He is the point man for our region and will take the rap if things go badly for Lintas.

But marital problems and trouble with one of his sons also weigh heavily on Lacour. An eye problem that his doctor cannot diagnose also disrupts his concentration, but Lacour agrees to the Harris plan.

Harris advises Lacour he'll be heading to Auckland with Greg Flint on Monday, September 28 to meet with a company lawyer they are about to appoint. Flint is the assistant to Bruce Marsden and has helped with accounting affairs in New Zealand. Flint has worked with David Downham and knows him well. Flint's help will be incalculable, because he knows where the money is buried. But in the opinion of the Murphy Truman group, Greg Flint is the wrong man for the job. Why concern yourself with finances when attention should be focused on keeping profitable business and getting staff back from the breakaway agency?

As Harris is in the final year of his thirty-two year career with Lintas, he advises Lacour in Paris and head office in London that recently-arrived Roger Neill should take the reins immediately in Sydney, rather than wait until the end of the year. It's agreed. Oddly, Roger Neill is the very man David Murphy had relieved of his wallet at the Connecticut leaders' conference as a bit of a joke. Neill, who looks and acts just like Murphy, right down to the moustache, will now be the big guy in Sydney. Maybe David Murphy should have been considered for that very job.

By Monday morning, September 28, (six days after the resignations) Harris is in Auckland with finance man Flint.

Mike O'Sullivan had arrived on September 23, one day after the break. He is informed about the breakaway at 10 am, two days ahead of the Sydney office? Why didn't he inform Harris, or did he? They are dark days for all concerned. Panic sets in.

Harris, Flint, O'Sullivan and Downham meet regularly in Auckland, to plot a strategy and sort out the mess. They still assume Downham is with them and has not joined the walkout.

On the first day in New Zealand, September 25, Harris appoints Colin Nicholson, QC, in Auckland to act on their behalf. Next Lintas, slaps an injunction on Murphy and me to prevent us from working on existing business. We are stunned by the move. During his first week in Auckland, Harris scheduled two other meetings with Nicholson to turn up the heat. The war is going to get messy.

The Lintas Goliath, part of the world's biggest advertising and marketing group, with billions of dollars in business, is going to do everything possible to crush us, because of a breakaway that might return $50,000 profit in the first year: that's it. It might cost them ten times that, just to destroy us.

But we scream, we are innocent; we just resigned, unfortunately staff and clients followed us out the door.

Portraying David Murphy, as the young Israelite boy opposing Goliath, the Philistine warrior, seems an appropriate analogy to us, it's no guarantee the small force will defeat the big one this time, but it seems an appropriate analogy for our supporters.

Murphy and I have the support of Tim Roberts and John Muir, our account directors, media director Mike Howard and David Russell, our production manager. David Downham, company secretary, and financial guy is still hiding in the Lintas wings At this point in time Downham could have remained loyal to Lintas and stayed with them, we are unsure. But at the time, this is our team at the new agency, along with a lawyer who will direct a defense strategy and combat the onslaught of legal moves coming from Lintas.

With the loss of staff and clients it must have looked to the outside world as if this was a well organized plan to destroy the office, but it is not. That is why we were so surprised by the swift and brutal moves. But what are we to do other than defend our actions?

Goliath, the team headed by Bruce Harris, will spend $20,905 dollars in staff time pursuing a case during the first three months, most notably an injunction followed by a lawsuit against Murphy and me for damages. His helpers are Marsden, Flint, Moxey, Webley, Spence, Scott and Gosling. Greg Flint is the worker bee for Harris. Max Gosling will come in near the end of the Harris odium. The others are primarily account clerks, but they all add to the team committed to our destruction.

Michael O'Sullivan will claim a paltry $1,157 in staff time pursuing the case. The above mentioned team is supported by Roger Neill, the new head of the Sydney operation, Jean-Francois Lacour and mister big, Chairman Tim Green, a key player on the International Board of Lintas in London. One hell of a team, determined to crush a tiny hard nut. *(The amounts stated are included in a "statement of claims" sent to our lawyer Mr. Graham, March 18, 1983, by John Gregory Collinge, Solicitor for the Plaintiff based in Auckland.)*

The biggest issue in law affecting our situation is labeled *fiduciary trust*. Lintas must establish that we've broken something sacred in British law, which means they must crush the nut before it takes root. Had we stolen property that will allow us to profit from products developed by Lintas? If we had it will be incorporated as new English Case Law and is likely to be quoted in future cases of this kind.

A DISAPPOINTING START FOR LINTAS

Harris and O'Sullivan do the rounds of every ex-Lintas client that intended to join the new agency, asking them to reconsider moves they are about to make, or have already made. Most make it clear they'll stay with the new agency. Some are prepared to give Lintas a chance to recover their business. Only Bendon decides to give up on both agencies and hand the business to another agency. *It is not good news for Lintas, as they are not welcomed with open arms as expected.* In fact, they are probably shocked by the dedication and loyalty New Zealand clients have for the people they've worked with in New Zealand, and not the international Lintas name on the door.

The travel, eating and accommodation expenses incurred by Lintas senior staff pursuing this case amounted to more than a *quarter-million New Zealand dollars.* Tim Green, the chairman of Lintas, in London, gave Harris carte blanche to do what's necessary *to win.* They believe they'll recover costs later, by suing Murphy and me.

THE FIRST STONE IS LOBBED AND IT HURT

October 1 –
Nine days after the resignations

Events move quickly. A legal document is given to us by the beginning of October, outlining the Lintas case against the two of us. When a court appointed courier hands us the legal papers, it's like a hammer on your thumb. The very look of the documents reeks of prison doors being slammed shut: it's all black and white like the stripes on prisoner clothing.

Bruce Harris, Michael John Fitzgerald O'Sullivan, managing director from the Lintas Wellington office and Cherie Suzanne Ryan, an employee of Lintas Auckland who didn't join the walk-out, provide details to the court as they saw them and they seem fair.

I have to laugh at one important detail. They incorrectly call me *"Dennis,"* when in fact my first name is Donald. They appear not to know my name, or who I am: typical of the fumbling by Goliath.

An interim injunction, which is a formal order issued by a court or judge ordering a person or group to refrain from doing something, a prohibition, has been delivered to us personally. This means they've succeeded in stopping us from working on all of the accounts that want to join the new agency, until 10 A.M., Monday October 12.

	Plaintiff
AND:	DAVID JOHN MURPHY of Old Coach Homestead, Kerns Road, Rama Rama, Advertising Executive.
	First Defendant
AND:	DENNIS RICHARD TRUMAN of 292 Victoria Avenue, Remuera, Creative Advertising Director.
	Second Defendant

No problem: it's only eleven or so days. It hurts, but is not terminal.

LINTAS THROWS MORE DEADLY STONES

October 1 –
Warrant to Sue for damages.

Next, a warrant to sue is issued. This is scary, but what does it mean? It means pretty well what it says: *Lintas is also going to sue us for damages, including loss of profit, loss of opportunities, legal expenses, costs from the upcoming trial and anything else they deem fair.* They can demand a million dollars in damages, we don't know. This can be a deadly blow, and in my case could result in financial ruin. There is no doubt that David and Anita will suffer a severe wallop as well, unless the new venture proves successful very quickly.

October 1 –
A Writ or Summons and Statement of Claim are issued.

This is the nasty bit. According to court papers we will have to pay the following if the court case is upheld.

(f) In respect of all of its cases of action aggravated damages against the First and Second Defendant in the sum of $50,000. (NZ dollars)

(g) In respect of all of its causes of action exemplary damages against the First and Second Defendant in the sum of $50,000.

(h) Directing that the First and Second Defendants pay the Plaintiff's costs of and incidental to this action and order or orders therein.

(i) Such further and other orders as this Honourable Court may deem just. (Including the cost of $300.00 for serving this writ and incidentals thereto.)

A CRUSHING BLOW HITS THE MARK

October 12 –
20 days later

By October 12, the judge must determine whether to extend the injunction or issue another order, which would mean we *would not* be able to make contact with any previous clients <u>for a period of three months</u>. In legal terms, it states (a) That the Defendants be restrained from approaching clients of the Plaintiff (old clients) and (b) That the Defendants be ordered to return property belonging to the Plaintiff. The Plaintiff had pleaded <u>seven causes</u> of action to support the application for the interim injunction. (based on the legal text provided by the court)

(i) Breach of Contract of service against both Defendants. It is alleged that the Defendants have:-
    (a) Failed to give proper notice.
    (b) Failed to act in good faith towards the Plaintiff.
    (c) Failed to work in the Plaintiff's interests.

(ii) Breach of Directors' fiduciary duty of care against both the Defendants. It is alleged that both Defendants in their capacity as Directors have breached their fiduciary obligations towards the Plaintiff in that they have failed to act in good faith towards the Plaintiff and failed to work in the interests of the Plaintiff.

(iii) Breach of confidence against both Defendants. It is alleged that information was supplied to the Defendants by the Plaintiff and the Plaintiff's clients in confidence. The Defendants have breached this confidence by using the information supplied to further their own business interests and to harm the business interests of the Plaintiff while still in the pay of the Plaintiff.

(iv) Inducements to breach contracts, against both Defendants. It is alleged:
    (a) That the Defendants induced the clients of the Plaintiff to breach their contracts with the Plaintiff.
    (b) Induced the employees of the Plaintiff to breach their contracts of service between the employees and the Plaintiff.

(v) Detention of the Plaintiff's property against both Defendants. It is alleged that the Defendants have wrongfully removed and obtained the property of the Plaintiff and that this property ought to be returned.

(vi) Injurious falsehood against the First Defendant. It is alleged that the statements by the First Defendant have impugned the advertising services provided by the Plaintiff causing pecuniary loss.

(vii) Conspiracy against both Defendants. It is alleged that the Defendants wrongfully conspired to:-

(a) Induce the clients of the Plaintiff to cease dealing with the Plaintiff.
(b) Breach their Contracts of Service with the Plaintiff.
(c) Act in breach of confidence.
(d) Induce breaches of Contracts of Service between the Plaintiff and its employees.
(e) Induce breaches of Contract between the Plaintiff and its clients.
(f) Improperly obtain possession of the Plaintiff's property.

THE ONE THAT HURT THE MOST

October 14 –
Recalled to the High Court of New Zealand

On October 14, Judge Holland agrees to slap a three-month injunction on us, and a mandatory injunction requiring us to return the goods we've taken with us. It's confirmed *they're going after damages in respect of all seven causes of action.*

The balance of the Murphy Truman Advertising staff will carry on business as usual, but the loss of our involvement is intended to create a strain between clients and our new agency. It might mean clients will walk from the new agency and drift back to Lintas.

It's a trying time, and for a short period has the desired effect.

The serious blows by the Harris team have weakened our self-confidence. Like two battered and bruised fighters, we go into hiding to rest and recuperate.

The mumbo jumbo of legal ramifications has our heads spinning, it is all so unfair, but we're determined to ride out the storm.

Bruce Harris and Greg Flint fly over numerous times from Sydney and stay off and on until the end of the year until they sort out the legal and operational mess and get the office up and running again. Harris meets with his legal counsel in Auckland on many occasions. He stays initially for two weeks, but comes back every second week, or whenever required, until the end of the year.

Harris believes his tactic of "spoiling and winning" is working. The "spoiling" is certainly working, but not the "winning." Lintas manages to retain both Feltex and Aulsebrooks, ONLY until the termination periods of one month and three months have expired.

Then, both accounts will join Murphy Truman. Lintas has nothing in the way of business: it has lost everything it wanted to retain. It too is suffering badly, but refuses to show it. Time is not on their side.

OUR MOLE IS "FLICKED"

David Downham, our mole, stays in the Lintas office at 100 Greys Avenue, reporting their moves to trip us up. We know what they are doing on a regular basis.

But, a careless move by Downham exposes him as *"working for the enemy."* Unfortunately, a Lintas employee spots Downham's car parked at the Murphy Truman offices on Anzac. Bingo. He's nabbed by the Lintas eye-hawks. On September 29, one week after the walkout, Downham is abruptly removed by Lintas and joins the new agency.

Lintas fires him by giving him what Harris calls, the *"flick."*

His Trojan horse reporting gave us invaluable information while the team from Sydney fumbled around trying to re-awaken a dead Auckland office.

Downham's title changes to general manager when he joins the firm, to ensure Murphy Truman operates profitably. His contribution will be invaluable, as he has a firm grip on the financial rudder from the moment he arrives.

The only ones left at the hollowed-out Lintas office are Cheri Ryan and Tracey Harbutt, two competent secretaries.

By now the Sydney office appreciated the tight-knit team that ran its New Zealand operation, and the loyalty of clients. The leaders in London and Paris ultimately paid a price for their long-term negligence.

Chapter 11

LINTAS HAS MOMENTUM & TAUNTS US

Newspapers follow the story closely. "Exodus from Firm Has Court Sequel," is the next big headline punched out by the news media.

The decision to extend the temporary injunction hit us hard. I lost momentum, believing I'd done something wrong and will be sued or imprisoned. Naïve, yes, but that is exactly how I felt.

A wonderful term, "a consensual reaction," sticks in my lexicon. It is a line a reporter threw at me during an interview. *"Was it a consensual reaction?"* It summed up so well what happened after we resigned. Emotions ran amok and everyone simply followed the leaders, including clients.

My biggest concern is for my family and our future. If this court case is spun without justice, and Lintas wins the battle, it can destroy my reputation and a lifetime of dedicated work. We are half-a-world away from home, have nothing saved. If things go badly, we'll have to sell our house just to pay our way home. Then, we'll have to start all over.

We cannot stop talking about the events of October 14, when Judge Holland recalled us to the High Court of New Zealand to announce his final decision, a decision that poked fingers in both eyes. The decision to extend the temporary injunction until December 22, 1981, stopped our spirited flit in its tracks. Harris and his team have an unfair reason to celebrate.

Judge Holland's comment that, "Murphy had been operating with some sense of bitterness…" – and "…it was clearly a scheme of avoiding tax liabilities," as reported by Wayne Garland in his *KIWI CAPERS* feature story, cut deeply and seemed so unfair.

But staying away from the office will allow us a little time to get out of the media spotlight.

LINTAS HITS THE FUNNY BONE

Shortly after, full-page ads appear in Auckland papers proclaiming, **"Lintas is alive and well and living at 100 Greys Ave."** The copy, probably written by Harris, states, *"In handing down his decision to continue the injunction against Messrs. Murphy and Truman on 14 October, Mr. Justice Holland of the High Court restrained the breakaways from any contact with all Lintas' clients until 22 December 1981.*

Now, for Lintas, it's back to business.

And it's business as usual at 100 Greys Avenue. Lintas continues in Auckland as a full-service advertising agency, with all the accreditations necessary to take care of its existing and new clients' affairs.

You might say we've been to the health farm in recent weeks, trimming off some of the fat. Now, we're lean and hungry; fighting fit; equipped to produce advertising that sparkles, startles and sells.

Call us. Come in and meet the team that has the extra enthusiasm derived from picking yourself up and dusting yourself down.

We're out to win for our clients as well as ourselves. – Bruce Harris, Chairman.

If you're a client of Lintas in New Zealand, what would you think after reading this pathetic drivel? Most left anyway, so I suppose it doesn't matter. They didn't like it at all. Many clients spoke to me after and chimed, *"It's no wonder ALL clients left Lintas to join Murphy Truman."*

The paragraph that has the phone ringing is, they've *"been to the health farm; trimming off some of the fat."* The fat that should have been trimmed is at Lintas head office and in its fat, dying-empire offices. It led to many chuckles over a beer.

Now a gang of "shipped-in" Aussies is going to be lean and hungry, fighting fit and equipped to produce advertising that sparkles, startles and sells! What blarney. What bombastic, pompous, verbose, long-winded, overbearing juvenile crap created by one of the world's greatest advertising empires. Overheads will now triple. It smacks of ignorance of the local market and another attempt to impress Lintas head office.

They believe the effect of the ad will be to encourage clients and ex-employees to return to Lintas, and attract new clients who might want to join the Australian-led, reborn Lintas agency. Tut, tut, it doesn't work. It's another rant to discourage the new Murphy Truman team, hoping we'll collapse. It doesn't work at all.

The wily Harris also arranges to put up a twenty-four sheet

poster to be installed across the street from our Anzac office, stating, "AD AGENCY WARS. LINTAS STRIKES BACK." Strikes back for what, we ask? Maybe it should have been strikes out?

Harris is in a rage, ready for the final battle. Why we ask, why doesn't he just talk to us?

From his point of view, he tastes victory and the news spread to Lintas International in London. But we didn't start the war, Lintas did. We were just caught up in a walk-out!

In his final 75 days at Lintas, the warrior is determined to nail the bastards with everything he's got. London has said, "Go get 'em Bruce - we'll pay the bill!"

The expansive campaign is, in our view, a waste of money, an expensive joke. It's embarrassing for a world-class billion-dollar organization to start a war with two little guys who had simply resigned. And in a fit of passion, all the staff and clients joined them. Once again, Lintas misjudged the mood in the country and the mood in the industry.

We're seen as locals; little David, brought to his knees by a one-eyed colossus, a multi-national bully with billions in the war chest.

Murphy Truman is Defiant

Murphy and I are resolute. We are determined to fight back. In our little kingdom, we are as indomitable as the spirited Londoners who survived the blitz and threw the battle back at the enemy. David's wine cellar at Rama Rama has many visitors about now, as we wade through the darkest hours in our underground exile.

The effect on business is negligible. Clients remain loyal. All but one of the staff stays and stability, even without our leadership, returns to the new agency. Our inside man Downham is back in the fold and provides invaluable leadership, along with John Muir, Tim Roberts, Michael Howard and David Russell. We hope these inside team members believe in us and become future directors and owners of the new agency.

The Press continues fulminating about the walkout, but the mood is shifting.

"It's head down at Murphy Truman," reports one paper, while another stated, *"New agency thumps out new shock."*

Murphy Truman is fighting back with the support of the local rags. But we're hoping the "dead hand" of overseas bureaucracy will tire, as costs spiral beyond reasonable.

The empty celebrations from the Lintas legal team can be heard across the city. But, the strategy of trying to keep us on edge and off balance is not working with our employees. Where the attacks do hurt however, is in encouraging the banks to question our ability to survive and prosper. Downham is pure genius at producing enough financial forecasts to build a bridge over troubled waters. We've gone this far and are dogged about responding with the unexpected.

The biggest surprise is winning additional new business while they're distracted, chasing their tails.

On an encouraging note, a white Mercedes, plate I Y3627, is delivered to my door as a present from Murphy, a bottle of 1979 French Beaujolais Reserve on the hood.

What more can I ask from my partner David Murphy, who is taking the big risk and is the one that will fall the furthest if something goes terribly wrong?

In the midst of this mess, Murphy also decides to lease a fleet of grey Datsuns for the staff. In another gutsy and popular move, he motors around town in his own classic green Jaguar. Another dream fulfilled. What a paradox.

When we met to celebrate, he's still spouting platitudes about the wonderful days ahead: no one is to worry, things will be fine.

This is the man Harris of Lintas recalls as a "a poor performer as far as profit was concerned, with an ego bigger than his abilities." Only time will tell whether they are right, but at the moment he has the absolute support of battered and bruised troops.

A ROYAL INTERRUPTION

Saturday, October 17, less than a month after our resignations, everyone is excited by a visit to Auckland by the Queen and the Duke of Edinburgh.

With nothing to do but await the end of the injunction, we put the family in our new Mercedes and journey to the Domain, a park in central Auckland, to see them. A thunderstorm strikes that day, and long does she reign, rain, rain, but it doesn't bother us. It's a sweet rain, with the aroma of fresh earth and promise that New Zealanders are used to. Huddled under our new Leopard Beer umbrella, we wait and enjoy the show. I can't take my eyes off my first Mercedes sitting on the grass, close to the stands. Down deep, I want to show it to the Queen and tell her I'm the owner, even though she's a friend of Rolf Harris, brother of Bruce.

The morning ceremony for the Queen and Duke is a Polynesian

welcome.

To warm up the crowd, the Royal New Zealand Navy band performs, followed by Mr. and Mrs. Piggy's appearance on stage. A truck load of ministers follows, with the usual huff and puff about love and loyalty. Finally, a *Karanga*, or ceremonial dance is performed after a welcoming *Haka*. The dancers slip and slide on the wet grass, giving the appearance of an amateur show. But the Queen doesn't laugh. The Royals remain cast in bronze and look marvelous huddled under their umbrella.

Then we all sing, *"Nau mai piki E to Kuinie,"* a welcome to our beloved Queen, prior to Mr. Piggy escorting them to an exhibition of ethnic arts and artists demonstrating native skills.

The dancers are dressed beautifully and represent some of the island nations written about in romantic literature: islands like Niue, Tokelay, the Cook Islands, Tonga and Western Samoa, islands and countries that impress with visions of peace and tranquility in a crazy world.

The children get wet. Beverley sits loyally, dreaming about her native land, watching every move. It's lovely. When it's all over, we rush to the Queen's wet Rolls Royce, hoping to catch a glimpse of her through the rain-soaked windows, and we do. Still clutching a small bunch of bright yellow flowers someone has given to her.

The Queen visits, the family rush to meet her.

But, I didn't get a chance to show her my new Mercedes. That would have made the day even more special for me. I'm still convinced she saw it sitting in the parking lot.

The weeks slip by but the dagger hangs in the air: we don't know where it will strike next.

By now, we're running all over the place, trying to get our daughters into private school. It seems that the thing to do if you live in Remuera is to get your children into private school so they can get to know other toffee-nosed (stuck up) youngsters. It's also good for business contacts and political connections. So, we apply to every school in the district and find just one spot available for our youngest, Nicole. We rush to the interview at Corran School. She's accepted. Unfortunately, that's it for openings this year. We'll have to wait until next term to enroll our oldest daughter, Michelle. But she's on the wait-list, and we're hoping someone will drop off.

Corran is just off Remuera Road, a little more than five minutes drive to school. It's a wonderful school with all the trapping of privilege and it felt right for us, because we live in Remuera. Without knowing it, we are becoming part of the upper class of Auckland society. Why, even the accents seem different. The posture is upright and we hold a cup of tea differently in Remuera. Nicole takes to it immediately and has to shed her blue dress for a handsome green uniform, including a green raincoat, a green leather school bag, a green school cap, and green, shiny shoes. Within a month she becomes school captain.

Nicole L Truman in Corran attire

There is something to be said for a special education with smaller class sizes and being surrounded by eager school friends. In little time, her marks reflect the difference as they reach new heights and stay there. In New Zealand, money buys opportunity.

Because we live on an island, the children are learning to swim. Nicole is studying music by learning to play the recorder, while Michelle is tipped by Mrs. Goddard, the music teacher at her school, as being a gifted violist.

It's not difficult for neighbours to look at us and believe we are doing well. After all, we're ensconced in a diplomat's home on an exclusive avenue in Remuera, driving a Mercedes and having our name plastered all over the local rags. Being in the papers means a degree of celebrity, but our friends know the story is much darker. But, we have to keep up appearances in Remuera and we must put our children first.

Celebrity in Remuera

The "Saga" Changes Course

Management magazine, a national magazine read by the pilots of industry, reported on happenings at Murphy Truman and Lintas in a story on page 12 of its November, 1981 issue, titled the *Murphy Truman saga*.

The report described the action after my resignation: "...like a run on the bank almost all the staff then followed in Truman's footsteps. As did most of the Lintas client list."

The article reported the old chestnut about the new agency setting up immediately. "The next day MTA set up shop in facilities in Anzac Avenue in conditions which were best described as frenetic. Certainly a far cry from the plush, refurbished office complex in Greys Avenue. To an outsider it appears to be work as usual. The atmosphere was vibrant, almost electric as management and staff ran an agency and created it at the same time. Bruce Harris, recently retired director of SSC&B Lintas' Sydney office and brother of the famous Rolf Harris, flew into New Zealand almost immediately to ensure that Lintas' abandoned Auckland office remained open, viable and operational – and that justice was seen to be done."

The story continued, "...So, in spite of the frantic legal actions of Lintas, a new advertising force is born."

By November, two months after the breakout, many in the media are sympathetic and provide support through telephone calls and personal conversation. They believe Lintas is dazed, heavy handed and careless and is only worried about its damaged reputation rather than the clients in New Zealand who might have been damaged by their miss-cued punches.

A song based on a popular hit, recorded and sung by the talented David Downham, suddenly appears. The lyrics are deep and cutting, what you'd expect with the emancipation of a subjugated business group under attack. It asks us to throw our fists in the air, march forward, defy the global giant: be freethinking and determined. The song is quickly released on audio cassette and many copies still float around today.

Thorn EMI tunes in

The best news of all is another new business win, Thorn EMI, two months after the resignations and the attack by Lintas. In the middle of an injunction, Murphy Truman is winning new business. The Goliath is stunned by the audacity of this punk breakaway group. I can hear Bruce Harris swearing about now.

It took business courage for Thorn EMI, a firm with reputable products and an international brand name to come on board an agency that is brand spanking new. The Thorn EMI account isn't small potatoes either. A number of national television campaigns have to be created as well as the usual clutch of ads, radio spots and promotional material. The momentum is contagious and marches us right out of trouble. The best news is that David and I are free to work on the account because it's not covered by the injunction.

Thorn has decided to market a number of small television sets for those inconvenient little spots where you want a TV.

Creative is a marvelous process when done right.

First, you digest all the facts about the market and the product. Then the brain takes over and processes thousands of bits of information. Then, you simply wait. Within hours, ideas spew out: it's amazing and it never fails. Never listen to the old wives' tails about dry spells. Good ideas tumble out every time, if you do it with discipline.

The first assignment starts with marketing three small television sets. So, we need a few words, nothing more than a few words. At the time, a television show called Three's Company is a big hit. In a few days, we return to Thorn with the campaign.

It consists of a photo of three TV sets in places where you might not normally find them, in a sailboat, in a bathroom and in a small study, because they're run by batteries. The headline stated, *THREE'S COMPANY.* Simple, but effective.

Despite the times, despite the horror of the Lintas attacks, the team still creates campaigns that deliver an effective punch in the marketplace. Within days, the ads, banners and promotional bits are in place and we're smiling for the first time in quite a while. What Lintas must be thinking never enters our heads this time. We've won this international account as Murphy Truman, so we roll right along.

Chapter 12

AN ANGEL OF MERCY

By late November of 1981, a glance at our client list is impressive. Big accounts like Aulsebrooks and Feltex are almost back (they fired Lintas and must wait for the one and three month termination agreements to expire before rejoining us) and still growing. Other national accounts like Continental Cigars, Dominion Television Rentals, Foodstuffs, James Hardie, Northern Roller Mills, General Foods and others are still with us. The most impressive are the international accounts destined for growth, such as Bendon, Leopard Brewery, Spalding, Club Med and, recently, Thorn EMI. Not a bad client list after just a few months operating our own company.

Buying media is one of the big responsibilities of agencies: everything from newspaper and magazines to radio and outdoor billboards. Our media director, Mike Howard, has been busy, as Murphy Truman has accreditation from most media. But we haven't been accepted by Television New Zealand to buy and sell television time, an important source of income, as TVNZ provides a whopping 20% commission to an ad agency. TVNZ, at the time, paid the highest media commission in the world.

Because of the bad press and the slap by Lintas, it's impossible to get approval from TVNZ to sell television media to our clients.

The situation is not good. It's a setback, because most of our clients need television time, fast. TVNZ is adamant and denies television accreditation to our months' old agency.

David Murphy has friends in the industry, developed over his ten years of agency experience. One is a senior adman, Bob

Wardlaw. Murphy has great respect for Bob, and Wardlaw in turn sees David Murphy as a bright light on the New Zealand ad scene. Their friendship is long and productive, filled with mutual support and, indeed, admiration.

Sixty-seven year old Bob Wardlaw has followed the creation of Murphy Truman Advertising. He offers to help.

He makes a move that is historic. We can get television accreditation, if Wardlaw buys the agency outright. Then, he can provide media services, including television, to all clients. It's a daring move and completely legal.

He buys a share of the Murphy and Truman agency for a dollar. He now owns the agency: everything is purchased, including the lease on the fleet of Datsuns. In reality, Bob Wardlaw Admarketing bought the share and then sold it to a group named Colson Marshall Developments Ltd., which (much later) sold it back to Murphy Truman when the injunction was out of the way. TVNZ approves television accreditation. *Detractors don't see this business strategy coming.* It is a completely unexpected twist of business practice that has heads shaking in the ad community.

It's one of the most audacious, yet clever, moves in advertising business history. It takes the stone out of the hand of Goliath, temporarily. The Lintas plan to recapture fleeing television accounts from Murphy Truman is lost to history. Once again, they've been outplayed.

Bob Wardlaw's television accreditation from TVNZ bails out the agency. He says, "...with a shrug of the shoulder our (Murphy

Truman) clients are now happy as we can buy television time for them," to the disgust of Bruce Harris, the tireless warrior. It's all legal and above board.

Wardlaw said, "I am satisfied I have done the best thing to make everything go well for everyone. It really is just a question of carrying on. I did not obtain any contracts with the arrangement. You don't buy advertisers. They go where they want to go."

On the Murphy Truman split from Lintas, the veteran of fifty years in the advertising business said if (the walkout) had happened to him, "I'd just have to accept it. Basically, because if something like that happened to me, I must have deserved it. I personally believe we must give a better deal to our (agency) account executives (like David Murphy). We are, after all, in the business of giving advice to an advertiser and that to a great degree depends on the ability of the (agency team) to give that advice." His views were reported by *Marketing* magazine, in its December-January, 1982 issue.

The *National Business* review got wind of the story and shouted **"Ex-Lintas executives sell out to Wardlaw agency."** Max Gosling, a Sydney-based director of Lintas in New Zealand, who is trying to sort things out, said, "…the accounts aren't up for sale," adding "…an agency is appointed by the client." Gosling also said, "It seems to me they are trying to get around it. We would have to ask our solicitors." Murphy commented in the same article that he felt the judge (in the original hearing) made a "very, very harsh decision," and that he was considering an appeal. He also said he's surprised at his staff's walking out in reaction. "You don't go around asking your staff what they think of you," he said. "They felt they were not working for Lintas, but for me." The same article also stated, "Murphy and Truman do not intend to return the files and artwork they have taken with them, when they left, because any order to do so was somehow omitted from the injunction. However, Lintas will be proceeding with a claim for damages."

Our angel of mercy, Bob Wardlaw, has made one of the shrewdest moves ever in the volatile advertising scene and it allows the agency to continue to operate while the principals rest and prepare for their return to the agency in January, 1982.

This move put the stone back in David's hand. This time, he flung the stone at Goliath's head, and stunned him.

CHRISTMAS WITH THE LIGHTS OFF

Activity is temporarily halted for the Christmas season. Business activity slows; in fact, it dies, during summer in New Zealand. The cities are deserted between the middle of December and the end of January, as everyone has gone to the country or is traveling.

Christmas lights are not a big thing either. It doesn't get dark until about eleven in the evening. Therefore, there's no reason to string up Christmas lights: there's no one still awake to see them.

Christmas trees, too, hardly exist as Canadians know them. But we go looking for a real tree anyway, children in tow, and return with what Beverley calls a "twig."

While driving around Auckland, elder daughter Michelle asks why Santa Claus' sleigh is being pulled by fish. Granted, it's painted on the window of a fish and chip shop. But, sure enough, the painting of the fat fellow shows him sitting in a sleigh pulled by eight giant fish. "Oh," I say, "there's something fishy about that!"

The twig follows us home that day and has pride of place in our vast living room. Then, we unpack Christmas decorations shipped from another time and a much darker place. Aside from a few balls and a rack of lights, there's no room for anything else on the tree. The twig looks sad and forlorn, so we buy cotton balls and sparkling stringers from the chemist to bring the tree to life. Hours later, it looks a bit like a traditional Christmas tree; more like a sad twig doing its utmost to get attention.

A failed Christmas Tree

No, the middle of summer doesn't look like Christmas; it certainly doesn't feel like Christmas, or smell like Christmas. It isn't Christmas. It's just too hot. The first Christmas in the British Empire is celebrated in New Zealand, a day earlier than in Canada. Hah, it isn't Christmas. So we give up and celebrate with a glass of sherry.

By Christmas Eve, we're ready to party.

We've been invited to a "barby" at the Yagusch's on Sonia Street, just around the corner. They've invited us to celebrate a southern Yule. We arrive, fire-up the barby, and throw chops, chicken wings, sausages and burgers on the embers. The sound of Christmas carols fills the hot air. Their tree looks better than ours, but still looks like a twig, so we have something in common. After an hour or so, we're not doing too badly; we're getting the spirit - straight from a twenty-sixer of Canadian rye whiskey.

The family will spend Christmas Day at Rama Rama, with the Murphys. David will understand. Hell, he's English, he'll appreciate us being starved of winter's chill and the squeak of snow. Our children can play on the water slide with their children, Matthew and Amanda.

Christmas morning, we're up at seven, to the sound of *The World of Christmas* in the background and the aroma of freshly baked mince pies emanating from the kitchen. It's difficult getting into the mood, even with carols, mouth-watering aromas and the excitement of the day. So much is missing thought, like the sight of the snow and brooding dark skies of a northern Christmas. How awful. We actually miss snow, freezing rain and seeing our breath, all part of the Canadian Christmas light show. With the aurora borealis gone, and no smell of flaming cherry from the fireplace, we'll miss the beginning of our seasonal hibernation. Just for one day, we pray, "Please snow."

The girls rush to the garden to pick fresh lemons from the orchard, for Beverley's gin and tonic. The short walk blows away any thought we have of enjoying our first southern Santa day. Like Bing, we are ... *Dreaming of a White Christmas*, but Burl Ives' *Frosty the Snowman*, and *Dancing through the Snow*, just don't apply. So, we gather around the tree and open gifts, but not with the usual vigour. We miss our families, they're so far away, and we miss our friends.

At ten in the morning we head to the Old Coach Homestead in Rama Rama. The journey is about an hour and we arrive in time to celebrate before Christmas dinner.

David and Anita greet us at the door and the Christmas of Christmases begins. It's a wondrous affair. Everyone is wearing shorts and sandals, with the exception of Anita, who is dressed fashionably in loose fitting beige slacks and a pretty white blouse she purchased in New York. Anita has invited her mum and dad, from Wellington, to join us for the annual celebration.

Celebrating Christmas at the Murphys'

Everyone arrives toffed-to-the-nines at the Christmas table, where turkey, cranberry sauce, roast potatoes and carrots are heaped high on generous plates. David carves the turkey while Anita attends to the rest. What would Christmas dinner be without wine? David rushes downstairs to the enormous wine cellar and retrieves the very best for the table. At least this part of the ritual of Christmas is familiar.

Once finished, the children rush outside to play on a water slide. On Christmas Day? It's a wonderful, generous Christmas and the Murphys have done everything possible to make us happy. But there we sit, Nirvanas of the north, northerners, somewhat lost in thought, perhaps dreaming of coloured lights shimmering on ice and snow, the sound of church bells and the smell of a crackling fire eating-up real logs.

So much has happened in twelve months.

It's a wondrous Christmas but we feel the difference: heat.

Chapter 13

ALL TOGETHER AGAIN

IT'S OFF TO WORK WE GO

By the beginning of January 1982, things are better for everyone. During the three-month injunction, David and I talked a lot about what has happened, and why. We each have slightly different views, but generally agree.

It started after we decided to set up our own agency. The only way we could do it was to resign. So, we did exactly that.

A few Lintas clients were told we "might" set up on our own one day. At no time did I hear David directly ask clients to join us. Nor did I ask for their help. In a few instances, clients did say, *"We'll work with the people we know."* That is encouraging, as we felt some might fire Lintas, give the usual legal notice and then join us in a month or so when it is legal.

Because of the potential initial heavy workload, we had to think about others who might join us in the new agency venture. It made sense to talk to the best, the two Davids, Mike, Jon and Tim. Frankly, we needed them. There is no pressure for any of them to quit; it's *their* decision. We could not promise anything but hard work and struggle as we try to build an agency. Resignations were not written in advance because we didn't know who would join us. Soon enough, we were wrestling with an out-of-control octopus. That's the script that is handed to us after we resigned on September 22, a little over three months ago.

As has been stated before, other staff didn't know about our resignations and were not advised of our plan to set up on our own.

Clients would have to decide whether to join the new agency after we'd resigned and cleared out. No agreements were struck, no guarantees were in place. They would make decisions on their own, if and when they pleased.

No side deals were made with any clients.

It all came back to a "consensual reaction." Everyone just piled on once it became obvious we were gone, an explanation never accepted by the Lintas giant.

With our passion to succeed, what else were we to do?

What happened is probably inevitable; it certainly is not a conspiracy. It is a bad reaction by Lintas management that started the dominos falling. Someone out there should be accountable. We have our theories. It certainly isn't Bruce Harris, or any of the Australian team who fought courageously to rebuild from the ashes. The finger points back to Paris, and beyond, for kick-starting a desire to set up on our own.

By January of 1982, Bruce Harris left Lintas to start managing his brother Rolf's entertainment business. Harris hates the thought of retiring. He's no slacker: he just wants to keep dancing to his own tune. Big things are planned, such as producing television documentaries with Rolf as host, and building his own investment company. His waterfront home in Sydney where he lived for over fifty years is the new center of his universe of activities.

Perth-born Harris will reappear at the final hearing, still months away. The final court decision is still pending and will take a year or more to reach the courts. Both of us will have to await the snail's pace of the law.

Lintas appoints Max Gosling to manage the Auckland office. Max is an Australian, and his appointment isn't appreciated locally.

Many Kiwis don't like being pushed around by Aussies, a situation a Canadian is familiar with when Americans try to dominate our conversation. British economist Arthur Seldon commented on big business, saying it's *"government of the busy by the bossy for the bully."* Bully is how I now label the Lintas behemoth.

Although heavily bruised, both of us go back to work on a regular basis when the interlocutory injunction is finally lifted on December 22.

The major accounts are ready to do business. Termination notices have expired and Lintas is notified it has officially lost both big accounts. Aulsebrooks and Feltex are at the door of our tacky premises on Anzac.

We owe a great deal of thanks to our tenacious clients who stuck with us through harrowing times, especially Bill Peake, of Aulsebrooks, and John Cameron, of Feltex. They suffered quietly and might have been the subject of ridicule within their own companies.

The sale of our company to Bob Wardlaw has been reversed and we're back in the driver's seat, owning Murphy Truman.

We're not yet free of legal entanglements, but the agency is successful, with millions of dollars in client business and one of the most exceptional advertising teams in the country. Not bad, and a reason to celebrate.

The fact that we're being sued for costs and damages is still staring at us from the dark shadows. Each of us is facing a lawsuit seeking more than a hundred thousand dollars.

Lintas' Wiggling Continues

Across the Tasman, Bruce Harris has every right to relax. He's achieved some of his goals. After this fiasco, he's probably thinking, *"My life is like a stroll upon the beach, as near the edge as I can go."*

At almost fifty-eight, Harris has passed stewardship of the Sydney office into the hands of Roger Neill. Harris is feeling good about his actions in stalling the Murphy Truman saga in Auckland. In short order, he's lobbed an interlocutory injunction as us, and set a damages lawsuit in motion to "keep us uncomfortable." But he must feel disappointed that no clients have returned to Lintas.

Lintas recruited one writer back to the agency, my associate creative director, Michael Forde. A nice man and a competent writer, he is frightened by the prospect of being shipwrecked on a distant shore, with no way of getting back across a wide sea to his home in England. No one blames him; it is a prudent move to protect his wife and child.

A feature story by *B&T Advertising, Marketing* and *Media*, page eight, reveals the mood in the Australian advertising industry about the case and has Harris feeling that he took the right action.

The big boots in the advertising industry, representing the largest agencies on the planet, have similar points of view and state it.

J Walter Thompson's Australian chairman, Pat Moran, says, *"I think Bruce Harris was damn right to do it. If I was faced with a similar situation, involving that number of people and that many clients, I would go after them all the way, and only New York could stop me."*

Bill Mango, managing director of Grey Advertising, comments, *"I say good on Lintas. More people ought to do that sort of thing. It's a very positive step and should give agencies more confidence to take similar steps, although it is always a traumatic experience. In similar circumstances, Grey would take similar actions."*

McCann-Erickson's Peter Charlton, chairman and managing director for Australia, says, *"I applaud Lintas's actions. I think it was an excellent response. Given the same circumstances, we would do it too."*

Michael Ball, vice-chairman of Ogilvy Mather International, after consulting O & M's lawyers about a memo he wants to send to all agency managers on the steps they should take when faced by a breakaway situation, says, *"The important thing to establish is whether there was any subverting (of clients) before the breakaways. In a free enterprise economy, an employee setting up his own business is a very healthy thing, but it must be done ethically. It must be open and above board. It is strictly unethical to canvass your employer's clients before resigning.*
I believe the Lintas case will give fresh enthusiasm to agencies to defend themselves legally against underground attacks."

The hornet's nest has been shaken by this article in the January 21, 1982 issue, written by Joeanne Hawkins from Sydney. The big boys in Sydney need to impress each other and their corporate bosses in London and New York that they are watching.

While under the injunction, I manage to prepare a detailed Procedures Manual (PM) for employees and directors. Everything is included: how to fill out standard forms, including purchase orders, memos and contact reports; details about what will be paid as expenses and what will not; advice on how to service the ten company cars, including David's FI 9857, my JR9855 and Julie Yonge's KD 5476 and mileage restrictions on leased vehicles. Holiday policies, time sheets, holiday pay and travel arrangement procedures are detailed to help keep a grip on costs.

All of the details in the Procedures Manual have been developed in consultation with various departments and with Murphy's input. It feels good to have such clear-cut control of costs. I for one never read such a comprehensive guide until years later while working with J. Walter Thompson.

CRACKERS, WOOL, AND FLYING HIGH!

By the end of January, 1982 we've something to celebrate. Business returns to normal, as the entire staff is back at the office. The only drawback is cramped office space.

Staff can be seen lying on the floor while doing business. Our producer, pretty Nicole Smith, with raven-black flowing locks, says the carpet *is* her office desk. Jon Muir is spotted sitting on a radiator, or curled up in the window box, reading a brief. At this moment, his office is "a section of wall." Papers are scattered about, taped to anything upright. A Snapits box is sitting next to a PAW lager can, which is holding down a pile of DTR creative ideas. Andrea and Julie, along with Beth and Linda, are running from here to there in our three offices, trying to keep up with activities. In isolated cases, they complete writing contact reports, while sitting on the "throne" in the girls' toilet. Art directors and account services co-mingle in the hallway; media planners and writers work on opposite sides of the same desk. All is joy and laughter, it doesn't get better.

Bill Peake from Aulsebrooks arrives. We review a pile of briefs delayed by the summer break. "It's not only exciting stuff, but it looks like fun," says Peake.

First project is a relaunch: take an existing Aulsebrooks product and make it look fresh and new. Huntley Palmer's Cream Crackers require new packaging and a new reason for women to buy them. This old standby is still the most popular cracker in the land, but is drying up in the market, being replaced by innovative products like crispbreads and flavored crackers.

Within a couple of hours, we agree on a new way to add sales appeal. In the new consumer speak, *"Here's a new reason to buy a cracker."* It's a wow and another reason to throw accolades at both the genius of the agency team and the skill of clients.

The campaign involves redesigning the packaging, giving it a bolder, brighter look on the shelf, and giving the appearance of newness: a repositioning.

We're suggesting they sell cream crackers as **an alternative to bread!** Not only is it simple, but Aulsebrooks doesn't make bread, so the strategy won't cannibalize another product in its line-up. It'll just take sales away from bread. The television and magazine ads scream the new positioning. HUNTLEY PALMERS CREAM CRACKERS – KEEP 'EM BY THE BREAD BIN - MUM.

John Cameron, the dapper, prof-like wonder man from Feltex shows up and briefs us on the launch of a new carpet. Cameron or "Camo" to his friends, is all stiff back and gentle talk, but as sharp as a razor.

The new carpet is called *Felted Wool*, which doesn't sound very interesting until he explains their designers discovered that the structure of New Zealand cross-bred sheep is ideal to craft a durable, tough, but attractively textured carpet. But, it's not a new concept, oh no. The Neolithic people from the Anatolia tribes of Asia have been doing it since 500 B.C. So much for new! But, it's really interesting stuff. Images of Neolithic people walking on carpets over twenty-five centuries ago rattle around in our creative minds.

With a collegial cry, we agree to call the carpet L'Afrique du Nord and we'll say Pierre Cardin inspired the colours and texture. What a sizzling fantasy to market the new carpet.

The budget for the launch is huge, with enough money to produce first class television commercials and full-page ads in newspapers and magazines.

A few days later, the idea for the commercial comes naturally.

We describe visions of a beautiful woman, wrapped in a flimsy see-thorough costume walking through a North African desert scene, conveying the mood and mystery of the region. Add a fireball sun, then a lush green oasis surrounded by palm trees and sand. The set is stylized, of course. The woman walks from the desert, onto the carpet, then dives into a blue oasis.

Add a spicy blend of modern Arabic music and we've created a dream-world cosmetic-style television commercial.

The resonant tones of Orson Welles will add the final touch of mystery to the images.

Expensive, yes, but I'm aware of the talents of Kiwis in design and set building, so I rush to Wellington to meet with designers at a huge film studio. The designer begins to create a fantasy set for L'Arfique du Nord. The set is the size of a football field and the artist's sketch envisions a beautiful fantasy.

A week later, we're ready to film the odyssey when the director yells, "Roll camera. Roll sound. Action!"

An unexpected problem arises as a ten-foot fan, used to blow wind across the set, removes the flimsy costume the model is wearing. In one take, she's naked. It is filmed, but, none of this ever made it to the final cut.

Pat Aulton, of Bogtunes in Sydney, prepares a music demo that captures the complex instrumental sound needed to support the mythical North African images. The demonstration tape leaves us breathless. I rush to Sydney to record the final score with musicians brought in from all over Australasia, then bring the "sound" track back to Auckland to marry with the pictures. Within a few weeks it's on the air, and Murphy Truman magic is on display for all the world to see and hear.

Then, it's on to a Hardies campaign, then DTR, Continental Cigars and a windstorm of projects that had backed up during our three-month hiatus, overwhelming the hard-working team.

It isn't long before Aulsebrooks is back with a bevy of new assignments, including the launch of a new crusty-bread product called Crispbread, and the second set of television commercials for the highly successful Farmbake cookies.

First in the production line is a new commercial for Crispbread, a large cracker, high in fibre but low in calories. The company will launch a new Cracked Pepper flavor to add to its successful Cheddar, Wheaten and Savoury lines.

Within a few months, Aulsebrooks experience another 32% growth, another example of the skill of the team under the management of Jon Muir and his Murphy Truman band. At the time I am thinking, *"Lintas, eat your heart out!"* Why would any company walk away from an ad agency that deliver results like this? They'd be nuts.

What is Lintas thinking? Do they expect a client to switch the account back to a bunch of strangers from Australia, simply because the name Lintas is on the door? It's the ability of the people clients want, not the international name on the door.

Thank God, Bill Peake of Aulsebrooks is no fool. Looking for a unique way to thank him, we decide to take him away for a few days to a gambling casino in Tasmania, just for a laugh. It's also a chance to do business in a unique location.

We fly to Melbourne, then hop on a short Ansett flight to Hobart, during a Tasmanian spring. Tasmania is the most southern state in Australia, with a reputation for allowing wild Tasmanian Devils to run free and as a holding pen for convicts back in the 1800s. Hell, they even sent convicts from the Toronto area to Tasmania in the late 1830s.

The real reason for the trip is to present Peake with a new television commercial for Farmbake, the fastest-growing product in Aulsebrooks' stable. He's unaware of our plan; he believes it's just a jaunt to have a few laughs. Maybe we'll present it somewhere between Auckland and Hobart, or on the way back, or somewhere unexpected in between. The underlying reason, really, is to thank this young buck for sticking with us through hell's gate.

Hobart is the capital of Tasmania, the only island state in Australia. No more than 400,000 inhabitants live in the entire state. Hobart sits on the south shore on the Derwent River, which flows out to the chilly Antarctic Ocean. Ships tie-up, in the very heart of the city, because of its deep harbour. It's a popular place for horny toads and sailors who rush here to whore and gamble. Sitting snugly near the harbour is the Wrest Point Hotel and Casino. This is where Peake will have a few drinks, chill out and gamble away twenty bucks or so.

After the usual round of drinks and throwing away twenty dollars, we tour the island, enjoying the twenty-one degree weather while scoffing lobster from cardboard plates in dumb outdoor restaurants. Don't see any Tasmania Devils, however. It seems 90% have been wiped out by what's called "Devil facial tumor disease". It's incurable and is spread by the little critters fighting each other and biting each other's faces.

David J. Murphy and Bill Peake

The other notorious Tasmanian devil is

Errol Flynn. The phrase, "in like Flynn," was coined to describe his sexual adventures. Oh, yes, there are many stories still in circulation today.

Captain Blood, one of the many Hollywood film characters Flynn portrayed, was born in Hobart in 1909. This swashbuckler led a fabled, perhaps debauched, life through three failed marriages and a bout with the bottle. His over-imbibing led to an early death in Canada in 1959.

Flynn is in Vancouver trying to sell his yacht, Zaca, to millionaire George Caldough when he fell ill. He is taken to the apartment of Dr. Grant Gould, brother of famous Canadian pianist Glenn Gould. Flynn reportedly said, *"I shall return,"* and retired to a bedroom to rest. Moments later, at age fifty, the swashbuckler is struck down by a massive heart attack. When he is buried, his buddies place six bottles of whiskey in his coffin as a parting gift. Our client, Bill Peake, looks a lot like Flynn, maybe a touch paunchier. And has that macho, horny-toad swagger local men seem to possess, probably in remembrance of Flynn.

The Australian penal colonies fascinate me, so I head along Convict Trail to Port Arthur. After an hour and a half journey, I'm staring at this huge and rather attractive yellowish four-storey prison. It looks like a warehouse, but started life as a timber station in the 1830s. Ten years later, the community housed 1,100 prisoners, primarily from Britain, with a few from Canada. It was a hellhole.

A splendidly written book by Australian Richard Flanagan, *Gould's Book of Fish*, recounts the sordid life of a prisoner in the Port Arthur penal colony in the nineteenth century. Van Diemen's Land, as Tasmania was known then, was hell on earth. When the tide from the Tasman rushed in, flooding the basement cells, the difficult prisoners usually sleeping in these cells would suffer a final water-torture. Unfortunately, they drowned during the night.

By the next evening, we are ready to return home. The only direct flight from Melbourne to Auckland is offered by British Airways, so we scramble to get on board. We're advised the flight has few passengers, so it's ideal. The rear area of the 747, ten seats wide, is almost empty. So, with the agreement of the crew and a couple of tired stews, we decide to make the presentation to Bill Peake. Peake will get to join the mile-high club, with a twist. No drinks: it's going to be a business presentation.

Within an hour, Bill is smiling ear to ear and breaks open a bottle of champagne as we celebrate another successful presentation and a significant new television commercial for Farmbake cookies gets approval to roll into production.

OFF TO THE STONEMASON'S

By early April '82, financial worries still stick to our skin like a cold sweat, but thanks to the skillful balancing of cash-flow by Downham and the co-operation of our bank, we're able to carry on. Running in the red is the short-term plan, but we know we'll move into the black one day soon. If cash runs low, we'll top it up by borrowing, and roll into April.

David Downham, a relentless fighter, is solid gold during the difficult days, as Murphy Truman has its mitts full with operational, new business and creative matters.

We have a problem providing adequate space; staff is finding it difficult to keep organized in squished quarters on Anzac. So, we swim deeper into red ink to find new digs. Daring and unconventional, we find a terrific location back where we started, in Parnell: lots of space, room for parking a few cars and a big barbecue area out back, for Friday night bonding.

After a lot of fretting, Murphy Truman is relocated to the Old Stonemason's House on Falcon Street, quite near our old offices. It's a breezy, historic, charming piece of New Zealand's early history.

Perhaps the greatest fun after the move is the client barbecues at four every Friday afternoon. Clients arrive, with bottles of booze, to enjoy the sun until we laugh the night away. Spirits are high. We're a professional operation, and we owe it to our clients.

A new phone system is installed, along with other new technology toys: 790-244 is soon ringing, with new business prospects.

New home for Murphy Truman

A defaced billboard

Then, our billboard down the street reappears and the defacing by other agencies starts up again. Not sure to this day who is behind the teasing on the billboard. It isn't Lintas for sure, but we're suspicious. It's a signal we've joined the human race again: we're back in the big league.

Our billings at this time are in the millions, placing us at number eleven in the New Zealand market.

By the end of April, 1982 I agree to buy 22,000 shares, with a par value of 50 cents, for $11,000 (NZ). The first payment of $5,500 is made in April 1982. The final 11,000 shares are purchased a little less than a year later, on February 21, 1983.

The par value, as agreed, is $5,500 NZ dollars, which gives me a 22% holding in the company. The facts are documented in correspondence from Graham and Company, dated September 28, 1982, as well as Certificates of Shares dated February 17, and 21, 1983. Not a lot in current financial terms, but at the time it is an astonishing level of personal investment.

The value of these shares will be disputed in future dealings.

By early May 1982, the family moves to a delightful Victorian-era house on Ngapui, not too far away. It has a large swimming pool surrounded by lemon and orange groves and a large grapefruit tree. It is wonderful returning home, peeling off the working togs and sliding into the crystal blue. The property has a huge tree house in the front, where the children hide and play after climbing the rope to their secret tree house, a well-appointed sanctuary. The house is just off Remuera Road and close enough for Nicole to walk to school at Corran, and for Michelle to stroll down Vicky Avenue to Victoria Avenue Primary School. Now, Beverley can walk to the wine store then shop along Parnell Road. It's a real treasure.

In a fit of generosity, the company loans me the money to buy a home. Murphy Truman Advertising borrowed the money, to be repaid once we sell our Canadian home, with the rest of our funds to be invested in the business. It is a wonderful fit of generosity by Murphy. With this move, came the requirement that we move quickly to sell our Canadian home.

It's also the time when we get serious about staying in Auckland, permanently. Young Michelle, at nine, really doesn't mind. Nicole, age seven, isn't sure what it means. My wife has reservations, but goes along with the family decision. I believe it's the right thing to do from a career point of view. But, we know we'll miss Trish Romance's version of Canadian winters and Christmas, and the changing colors of the seasons as painted by Canadian artist William Campbell.

The biggest problem looming is the slap of justice to be faced within the year, no matter where we live. So, why not settle permanently here? We're ready to fight the unfair legal actions to be delivered by Goliath.

We must return to Canada, in May 1982, just after Nicole's birthday, to get things rolling on the sale of the house in Toronto. Chances are we'll sell it at a good profit. Our trip will allow time to say goodbye to my parents, Webby and Annabell, and my brothers Bob and Harry and sisters Joyce and Marion. Beverley, an only child, will have the toughest challenge of all, saying goodbye to her father, Charles Holland, who lives alone in Eltham. Then, we'll return with money in hand.

Despite our careful planning, an unexpected tragedy half a world away will upset everything.

Shooting in the Wheat Fields

Back in the ad biz, filming is about to commence on one of the largest scale productions we've ever encountered. But this is New Zealand, where the law insists everything must be produced locally, so we get on with the task. The Murphy Truman dreamers and doers are *gaga* at the challenges, unaware at this point of the enormous and unexpected bonus that will catapult the agency into the stratosphere.

This is the campaign Bill Peake agreed to while traveling from Melbourne to Auckland in the back of a jumbo jet a few weeks earlier.

Farmbake is the largest-selling cookie in the country and we're about to embark on phase two of a massive new television campaign designed to boost sales even further. The slogan "Farmbake, A Taste of Home," and the campaign concept have been a hit for over a year.

The idea of fresh-scrubbed public schoolboys, away from home, getting "fresh" cookies from home is in play. The idea is loved by the mums of the islands, who cannot get enough of the storyline, seeing their sons as privileged school kids away at private schools, receiving cookies that taste like home baked.

School boys boarding a train, heading home from Wellington, will be filmed: a train load of school boys, excited about seeing their mums, dads, brothers and sisters is like a saccharine chapter in a soap opera.

The image of the train chugging through golden wheat fields says "from farm-fresh grains."

At the end of the commercial, a boy is seen stepping from the train in the mythical town of Hedgewood. He's greeted by his mum, sister and his dog, Woof. The camera follows his tentative first steps as mother and younger sister rush to greet him. They're overwhelmed by emotion. It's a scene from a sugarcoated '50s movie. Tears flow as they embrace. The other boys on the train wave goodbye and smile as they depart for the next village. What's this got to do with cookies? Well, nothing. But it works.

The script calls for a cast of a hundred and a fully operational train, which the railway will have to pull from service and rent to us for a day. The Wellington station has to be closed overnight and the train must be filmed running through New Zealand wheat fields. Then, we'll film interiors, with the boys playing. And, we have to find an abandoned railway station to paint and redecorate to become Hedgewood station.

No problem in Hollywood, but how can we pull it off with a limited budget, and no train in sight?

Oh my, Kiwis love a challenge.

First, we must find a production company. Then, locate a good director and producer and leave the locations, casting and timing up to them. Interfilm Wellington is selected, along with director John Blick and producer Norman Elder.

It's Friday, and I'm off for a beer with the agency creative types and producer Nicole Smith, who is on the case. We're excited.

Aulsebrooks, labeled the *Original Ideas People*, is pumped about Farmbake. The fan mail is a torrent of rave reviews from thousands of mums around the country. It seems with every thousand letters from happy mums, a new flavour is added from Peanut Crunch, Fruit and Spice, Marmalade, and Chip Nut to Shortbread and Chocolate Cherry. Demand soon outweighs supply.

In a trade magazine feature headlined *"Big homegrown success story,"* Bill Peake, the marketing manager, wrote about the phenomenon this way. *"Yes, yes, yes, we've found a successful and powerful formula for our advertising, and we'll continue to develop it. The schoolboy, away from home, has met with instant approval and adulation by the mums of New Zealand. The letters we receive are heart-warming, and continue to prove that you don't have to yell, scream or insult the consumer's intelligence through your advertising."*

This is a phenomenon that registered on the Richter scale and will one day be in the Marketing Hall of Fame. It's a soft sell that struck the heart unexpectedly.

Finding dinosaurs

Dinosaurs still exist. I'd read in the *"New Zealand Endangered Species"* publication that they still live in New Zealand, somewhere around Rotorua, in the middle of the north island. As we're going to deliver a kitten to a customer in Rotorua, here is a chance to see a real dinosaur walking the street. I now have a challenge: find the dreaded *Tuatara* and show it to my two daughters.

I'm so angry I'm thinking, *"I can shoot it, write Harris' name on its back and mail it to Bruce Harris in Sydney."* I cannot escape from the anger I'm feeling about the financial blow headed our way.

This dinosaur, native to New Zealand, is the most ancient of all living reptiles, even older than the popular, extinct dinosaurs. It has survived for almost 200 million years. This one is a tough little bugger that can live up to 100 years.

It's easy to identify them: they have beak-heads and three eyes, one on each side and one on top of their heads. The top eye is covered by hair. If they want to look up, the hair stands

The last dinosaur

straight up and they look straight up through the hair. The third eye is only used in an emergency. They're like lizards (20" long) and supposedly live around the mud flats in Rotorua, exactly where we are heading. But do they devour kittens?

The sun rises on Saturday. The kitten is ready to deliver to Mr. Toade. He insists we hand deliver the kitten and discuss the idiosyncrasies of the Burmese breed, face to face. Beverley knows cats, as she's now an assistant to our local vet. Therefore, the challenge is not a difficult one.

But business being business, I do the math. The kitten has a market value of about $200. Our expenses to drive to Rotorua, and stay the evening at a local hotel, feed the family and visit the fabulous mud geysers amounts to well over $350. Hey, that's a loss of $150. But, if we're lucky, we might find a dinosaur, too.

It's a beautiful journey through enchanting valleys where the Jolly Green Giant probably lives, until we near Rotarua and encounter the stench of sulphur. If you like sulphur, it's heaven. But if you don't, it's a smell that will bring on a headache or two. Because we love the look of the squirting, bubbling mud geysers, we put up with the stink.

Michelle, Nicole and I look for the Tuatara, with no luck. I ask a few locals, who stare back with disbelief. "What?" they say. "Never heard of it."

Tracking down a Tuatara in the jungle

The kitten is delivered, then we drop into our hotel and spend the day looking around the geysers for the Tuatara. Swoosh, gush, the grey-brown mud hurtles into the air as if managed by a clock, but no sign of wildlife.

On the way home, the children decide to sing a song they learned at a charity drive in Auckland. *"Thank you very much for the kind donation, thank you very much, thank you very very much, thank you very much for the kind donation. Thank you very, very, very much...."* There is no end to this song. Years later, we recall all of the lyrics and even the melody. But the song is so annoying when sung repeatedly.

The children have a wonderful time in Rotorua, but don't find the promised dinosaurs. And losing more than $150 on the sale is a lesson in business smarts. With the distraction of a song sung over and over, familiar to all parents with small children, I get lost coming home, nearly impossible in this wondrous little island. We arrive just in time, before our heads explode.

I was so annoyed no one knew about the last dinosaur I went to the Auckland Domain Museum in search of an answer. After all, they too had told me about this mysterious monster.

Tuatara means "old spiny back," in Maori. And sure enough, *the three-eyed monster is still alive.* They now live on the thirty-two south islands at the bottom of the country because it's cooler. They were chased from the mainland by predators, particularly the Maori rat (Kiore). I'm delighted that a few live in protective custody in a bush area at a museum in Invercargill - sadly only a few still survive.

They don't eat kittens either. They prefer baby mice, moths and beetles.

The Farmbake extravaganza we're about to film falls into shape rather quickly. Wellington station will close and the opening scene of the boys saying goodbye to their headmaster will be filmed at night. Parents and supervisors from the private school that provide the cast are told it will be a full day of filming, ending during the night at Wellington station. A train is taken out of service and booked, complete with an engine, four carriages and a crew that will operate everything according to their rules, not ours.

A fifth carriage, with shakers, will be placed in Wellington station for the interior filming. Shakers are men who shake the train to give the impression of movement. If you are inside looking out, blue

screens are placed outside the train windows to look like sky; tree men rush by the windows with tree tops in-hand, to make it look like the train is traveling at a high speed. It looks dumb while filming, but looks magnificent in the commercial.

The wheat fields, with the full train traveling through them, will be filmed the next day, which will mean more travel for the crew and cast.

The boys chosen for the commercial are from one of the more privileged private school in Wellington. The school will receive a donation, but no individual students or parents will be paid.

The rest of the cast will come from the feature film talent pool in and around Wellington. As this is a full sixty-second commercial, a lot of footage will be needed. The music will be performed and recorded later by an Auckland orchestra, once the edit is complete.

By the end of filming, editing and adding music, it's one of the most professional shoots ever managed. With the assistance of producer Nicole Smith and Interfilm, it's wrapped in days, on budget and on time. The sun remained loyal and weather insurance didn't have to be activated.

Not only is the campaign a hit in the marketplace, but within weeks the commercial earned worldwide acclaim for the agency by winning a Clio award in New York.

"Winning" is the point. *"It won,"* we scream in disbelief. It's an enormous achievement: recognition that we're as good as, or better, than anyone on the planet. We have been recognized by the world and we celebrate like never before.

Chapter 14

"DOWNHAM - I JUST CAN'T DO IT"

Nothing succeeds like success, and we're wallowing in it. It's like visiting heaven and hell on alternative days. On the good days, with ringing success, we're celebrating too much and Murphy and I are guilty of displaying ego, with a touch of arrogance, but neither of us realizes it. Self-importance, self-esteem, according to the dictionary, means, *"...devoted entirely to one's own interest."* Oh, oh, this feels dangerous.

The poor bloody ego has a hard time serving three harsh masters.

The Canadian dictionary says *"seeking the welfare of oneself only; selfish or talking too much about or thinking too well of oneself; conceited."* Best described as something intuitive: buried deep, but devoted *to one's own interest.* Not very promising, but it's a state we might have slipped into.

Instead of thinking things through, we grab the first suggestion and run with it.

While a marketing solution is the first step in a plan - an advertising solution that will win *awards* might be an even better alternative.

There is too much drinking and self-congratulation. Drugs slip into the agency, ever so slightly, through one of our suppliers. I was there. Not a big deal, but it's chipping away at a solid oak base. Maybe we're running away from the facts facing us. So, with an incredibly good reputation, we begin to place ads that blow our own horns.

But, on the bad days, fear of the damages lawsuit prevents us from being swallowed by our bulbous egos. Because we own the agency there is no one else to watch us, or complain about decisions. We rely on our judgment and our instinct and that is dangerous.

As it's time to chase new business, we place daring double page screamers in the Australian and New Zealand trade papers.

The first ad said, *"Twice upon a Time,"* and chronicles the birth and history of the agency and why it has been a smash hit. The ad is subtitled, *"Murphy Truman Magic."*

A second in the series follows, revisiting the success of the Aulsebrooks line of products, and is a tribute to the electricity generated when two people with great alchemy burp up award winning answers to complicated marketing challenges. It shows the two of us as chefs baking up a new solution and said, *"The ingredients for success – Murphy Truman magic!"*

Rubbing the right people together does create sparks, and we've started a blaze.

GLOBE HOPPING TO TROUBLE

In June 1982, the family leaves on a well-earned two and a half week vacation, or a trip back to Canada to sell the house and say goodbye to friends and family.

The first stop is London, where I catch up on news about Canada. It isn't good. It appears the country is suffering through a near depression-era recession and the bottom has fallen out of the housing market. Correspondence from friends had hinted at a problem, but nothing of this magnitude. Beverley's father is the first to talk about the reality of life in Canada. Mortgage rates are 22%, he said, and houses don't appear to be selling. He believes if we sell we'll lose money, so he warns against it. Our house in West Hill could lose 40% of its value. At first, I'm a little suspicious, as I can understand the emotion of a father about to lose his only child to a country half a world away. He has every right to be concerned and not want her to make a move with his only grandchildren in tow. Alarm bells have gone off. We're in a state: it's obvious there is a problem, but we agree to wait until we get to Canada to make a decision.

In 1982, Canada records its first case of AIDS.

Glenn Gould, the famous Canadian pianist and brother of Dr. Grant Gould, the man who was with Errol Flynn when he died, passes away.

John Robarts, the ex-premier of my home province of Ontario dies, as well as Russian spy Igor Gouzenko. The news is bleak.

The economic collapse is dreadful. Beverley and I know, that day, there is no way we can sell our house in Canada. If we do, we cannot afford to buy our New Zealand home, the one we're living in, nor can we make the necessary investment to keep Murphy Truman alive and breathing.

The net worth of our Toronto property might be only 40% of its purchase value. The news is unexpected and is shattering dreams. Our world is turned upside down and there is nothing we can do.

Cannes and can'ts

Before leaving New Zealand, I had arranged to meet David Downham at the Cannes Film Festival in the south of France. It's the festival of festivals for advertising agencies, competing with each other for world recognition: Golden Lions, Silver Lions and Bronze Lions and a bucket of other awards rain down on the globe's best advertising commercials, and the best agency people. I know: I'd won a Bronze Lion while working in London. After winning a couple of awards at Cannes, writers and art directors raise their incomes to phenomenal heights. For us, 1982 is the year to be an observer as we have not entered any commercials in the festival.

So, my flight plan has me traveling from London to Cannes to meet with Downham. But, my heart is broken. My luff is flat. I will remain quiet and keep the news to myself.

Egos are on display as we flash the bucks as if there were no tomorrow. We spend a couple of days watching the best commercials in the world. Most of the stunners are British, with a few French and Australian winners, along with a token effort by New Zealand agencies. But we're buoyed, and mumble about next year being the time to enter our best, to see if we can compete with the big stars.

We have specially made jackets with "Murphy Truman Cannes 82" stitched in big letters on the front. We look smart and give the

David Downham at Cannes

appearance of a world class agency.

But, I'm depressed and wrestle with the idea of talking to Downham about the dilemma.

Delay is my tactic, knowing I must wait until I return and talk directly to Murphy. Downham will return directly after the festival, which means he'll be back in Auckland ahead of me. London is my next stop, to meet with the family prior to continuing our journey to Canada, then flying back to New Zealand.

The last morning, while sipping tea at an outdoor restaurant at Rue de Canada and Boulevard del Croisonte, I spat it out without much thought, "David, I just *can't* do it," and asked what he thought. Downham paused, thought a little, and said, *"Oh, oh!"* then changed the subject. I suspected he wanted to think, but I knew exactly what happened. The future of the agency is in doubt, with one of the original backers pulling out because of something he can't control. When your name is on the door, you're a big partner. But maybe it's not as bad as I've been told; maybe there's a solution that Downham and I can work out.

That beautiful, quiet morning, distracted by the Cannes beauties strutting their candy, the deep blue sky, the froth on the Med, a scene that knocks ten years off your life, I'm stunned by his reaction. He doesn't want to talk, so I tune out. Downham knows what will happen and so do I, but I want to talk with Murphy first. It is too late, as I suspect Downham will return to New Zealand and tell Murphy the news first that I cannot sell my home in Canada. Without the sale of my home, there will be no money to invest in the business and I will not be able to stay in the home the company has just purchased in Ngapui for the family in Auckland.

In a beautifully choreographed dance of shoe leather and flying wheels, I land at Heathrow's terminal three, walk a few paces to the Air Canada lounge for a connecting flight to Toronto, and there they are. We rush at each other flush with excitement. Beverley and the children arrive from Eltham (where they stayed while I flew to Cannes) right on the money and we embark on an awkward journey to Toronto. After discussing the situation with Downham with my wife, she says, *"He'll tell David as soon as he gets back. I don't trust David Downham."* Simple logic from a clear-thinking wife!

In Toronto, we meet with the West Hill real estate agent to arrange to sell our house. The warning from friends and family becomes reality the moment we meet: things are bad.

Tom Rivers has moved on and the house is rented to two Indian families recently arrived in Toronto. It smells of curry. Two large burn spots on the basement floor indicate someone had cooking fires of some kind. The roof is a mess. Neighbours tell us two older children lobbed pointed darts over the house as part of a game. Most landed on the roof, ripping into the summer-soft roof tiles.

We are furious. The value of our home has plunged. What we heard in London is true: the market is a mess. Our friends are also concerned about the value of their homes. The real estate agent says we can't put our house on the market until the roof is replaced and the interior repaired, which is going to cost, cost, cost. Aside from shouting at the rental agency and threatening a lawsuit for not taking care of the property, little else can be done. And we decide not to sell the house.

With brave faces, we carry on. It isn't the time to say goodbye to family and friends. The only utterances are, *"We think we're coming home!"* Friends suggest we think it through. There are no jobs and the economy is in a nosedive, so we might be better off staying in New Zealand. We keep our brave faces and carry on: it's too complicated to explain to them.

Next stop is "Hollywood," as my daughters call Los Angeles Airport, where we board an Air New Zealand "big blue" for the six-hour ride to Hawaii. Flying business class on sheepskin seats makes the journey easy. I say hello to my first bottle of Hinano beer, from Tahiti. Although we've nothing to celebrate, we still enjoy the moments to relax, enjoy business-class food and the evening light out our window.

In Honolulu, we receive the traditional Hawaiian leis to fling around our necks. Not plastic. Fresh, fragrant flowers symbolizing a bridge to the ancient Hawaiian culture.

The first day is the hottest on record. The beaches are deserted. The hotel room is sweating on the inside. The moisture is so thick we can write our names on the windows.

While relaxing, the family attend numerous ceremonial dinners, featuring pigs cooked in the traditional way. We watch dancers do the hula, a Hawaiian celebration of life. According to history, Pele, the Hawaiian goddess of fire, created the hula as a means of passing along stories and legends from one generation to the next. We quickly learn the hula, how to chant, and why Hawaiians visitors throw *leis* in the ocean. If the leis come back to shore, it means visitors will return to these pretty islands. Without thought, we throw ours into the ocean, in the hope we'll return one day. They do return to shore, and drift onto the rocks below.

A week later, tanned and rested, we board the long flight to New Zealand. This entire journey has been paid as a business expense of Murphy Truman. I appreciate the financial advantages of being an entrepreneur. Business expenses allow considerable freedom of interpretation, if presided over by good accountants. I like it and indulge in it for the rest of my working days.

But on the somber journey back to Auckland we agree life has taken a one-hundred and eighty degree turn, to the north. Murphy, by now, will know about our financial problem. Not only do we face problems in New Zealand, but now we face security problems in Canada. There is nothing to go back to, no job and a house losing its value daily.

We arrive in Auckland and return home.

The next morning, I go back to the office. I'm not sure how Murphy will react. It's a troubling time, especially for the agency lynchpin. He's a trusted partner. I have let him down; really let him down.

When we meet, he dismisses my personal problems, believing I've simply made a decision to back out. To me it is simple, the recession in Canada that year means we can not sell our home without a substantial loss, therefore my plans to move permanently to New Zealand are over as is my plan to invest in the agency at this time. Murphy has every right to balk, but I do not think he believes me. I had not voluntarily changed my mind, a recession had.

From that point on, he and a few others begin to distance themselves from my problems and me. What had Downham said? I do not know, and it's never explained. Murphy is upset that I had decided not to sell my Canadian house. I cannot blame him for his fury. What would I do if the shoe were on the other foot?

His bruised ego kicks in and he's about to charge ahead, confident he can do both jobs: be a marketing strategist and a creative dreamer. Murphy is a brilliant strategy man and a gung-ho marketer, not a creative guy. We reach an agreement to move on and I agree to delay my departure and the sale of my shares until a time more suitable for the agency. But the smoldering resentment remains. Our relationship has been fractured. We have no choice but to move on.

Murphy Truman must find a new writer. I will have to train that person, while I arrange to get the children back to a Canadian school before September 1983.

The nightmare haunting us now is made worse by the bloodied hand of the Lintas damages lawsuit that looks as if it might crash down on Murphy alone. I disagree. I believe they will go after both of us, but he is unsure and frightened. And dear Anita, David's wife, is also on the hook for the biggest gamble of our lives.

Ngapui gone – Victoria's back

The first move is to sell our new home on Ngapui and move into a rental on Victoria Avenue, not far from the original home, at the end of a long downhill driveway. The house is ultra modern; the garden surrounding it is filled with aromatic honeysuckle, holly bushes and ivy vines.

Walking in a straight line from the front door, across Victoria Avenue, I arrive at my little corner IGA store. Nothing pretty, but it is packed with goodies. It has everything for the last minute shopper, including a quality butcher. The big delight is Tip Top ice cream, made with delicious New Zealand cream. By the time I walk down the hill, the children are ready to indulge.

On the way, I pass another neighbor's stately home. Draped over the sidewall is an enormous passion-fruit tree, with branches cascading down to the ground. The luscious dark-purple fruit is ripe, ready to be plucked. You simply slice it open and scoop out the mushy, guava-like sweet pulp. Oh, what a target for anyone savouring a fast dessert; my sticky fingers led to many thieving runs on this Brazilian transplant.

The house belongs to a government financial guy, George Luszczewski, and his pretty wife, Brenda. She's a pediatrician. One day, Doctor Brenda appears at our front door. They spotted me raiding their passion-fruit tree. Brenda, although somewhat shy and timid gets to the point, "Please be aware that unripe passion-fruit can be toxic." It's merely a warning. She doesn't want the children getting sick from her fruit. "If it smells of cyanide when you slice into it, throw it away," she says. "After abscission (cutting off), the fruit matures and shrivels a little," she says. "That's the only signal the fruit is ready to eat."

The Luszczewskis become good friends as we share wine and cheese regularly, about once a month. They're a delightful couple, with something of interest to say every time we meet. George is the only person I know who mixes Coke with his wine. They're great neighbors, even if we over-indulge on occasion and fall downhill walking home. They are cat fanciers, too, and have an Abyssinian, named Abby, who is never let out of the house. Abby just sits in the window, playing mind-games with our two cats.

The other neighbors immediately next to us are the Gillettes, distant relatives of the founder of the Gillette razor blade company. They become good friends, too, even if they do make the world's worst pizzas. Victoria Avenue is a lovely neighbourhood, and in short order we don't miss the activity on Ngapui. But, we do miss the swimming pool surrounded by lemon and orange groves. Soon the plan to own a home in New Zealand evaporates like ice on a hot day, the move is a slam-dunk – the dream is over, we're back to renting property on Vicky Ave.

With the pressure to settle the damages lawsuit still ahead, we know we have time before we have to face the courts and argue our case. If business remains strong, we might earn enough profit in the first year to *settle* the financial demands they might force upon us.

Now is the time to hire a new writer. I fly to Sydney with David to hire a replacement for me. Since Michael Forde, my previous writer, returned to Lintas, it's been a struggle keeping on top of business growth. We're still running lean. A writer with the necessary touch is needed to become familiar with client business, before pushing *her* into the spotlight, knowing *she* must take over. There are too many men in the senior ranks, so the addition of a woman is a clever business strategy. After all, women buy most of our clients' products, so it made sense.

A good female writer, ready to join in a month, is corralled. The position is attractive. One day she could become a partner, too. It's not out of the question. I soon discover something distressing however, that lead to complications. The signals are there but I don't notice. She is good-looking and saucy; that's the problem. How could I have missed the fact that temptation might lead someone astray.

In a couple of days, we're back in Auckland. The Cream Crackers campaign, is another big hit with the slogan, *"It's a Snacker of a Cracker,"* and quickly moves into production.

The biggest campaign, however, is the second half of the phenomenally successful Pierre Cardin carpet launch for Feltex. With this million-dollar baby just ahead, I'm temporarily distracted from the fight with Lintas.

With expanded egos and a new writer ready to join, we're set for the challenges. But my relationship with Murphy is still strained.

Word is out that Bruce Harris, of Lintas, is prodding the New Zealand courts to get a rapid summary for court action. That's worrying, as a delayed decision might allow us enough time to complete a profitable first year and settle the damages lawsuit with cash in hand.

Reports in the papers about the case persist; our successes and failures seem to titillate readers. The stories are interesting and everyone wants to know when it's going to be over and who will pass Go or be sent to jail.

By now, I sense the local agency scene sees Murphy Truman as heroes and Lintas as the big international bogyman. We are slowly winning the press war.

"LINTAS WALKOUT – HAVE THEY GOT AWAY WITH IT?"

In the winter of 1982, an article appears in *Advertising News*. Its tone sent the wags at Lintas into a tail spin. From the content of the article, written by Jeremy Light, it appears we got away with it.

It develops a thought someone has passed along to Light.

"Agencies must be able to continue working, admittedly, but it seems surprising that they (Lintas) have almost stopped fighting the men that emptied Lintas Auckland.

The article continues:

"Apart from the usual upheavals of business and staff, the news from New Zealand's agencies since September has been dominated by what has become known as the Murphy Truman walkout.

As an outside observer, it seems extraordinary that the result – that Murphy Truman Advertising – should be accepted, rather than tolerated, in the way that it is. <u>Its principals did, after all, strip Lintas Auckland of all its staff and clients (worth about $3.5 million.)</u>

As walkouts go, it is a particularly devious one, yet court cases that went against Murphy Truman Advertising, refusal of its accreditation and general industry condemnation have not halted the new agency's progress.

Now that most of the dust has cleared, there is little in the way of public outrage except a regular defacing of the agency's ad on its billboard site at the bottom of Parnell Road.

The agency looks set to survive, unless a damages lawsuit by Lintas goes ahead successfully.

The other extraordinary aspect of the walkout is that no one was prepared to criticize the clients that supported Murphy and Truman in their coup, or even Bob Wardlaw Admarketing (which is helping by handling the media placement).

<u>*While the whole affair has been watched with interest by industry observers from around the world, it clearly has not been good for the industry in New Zealand.*</u>

Maybe this has been the reasoning behind the industry's decision that it now is water under the bridge and the issue should be dropped so that everyone can get back to work.

Even Lintas has decided to keep the legals down to a minimum and concentrate on advertising. Swift work by overseas executives (Bruce Harris in particular) and a commitment to rebuilding have seen the office get back to about half its original size."

That pretty well summed it up from an industry watcher's point of view. But, from our sight line, the battle could end with a financial bruising. Which is contrary to what the press has been reporting. Either we fire up the engines before I return to Canada and make a significant profit, or Lintas will have its day.

Chapter 15

THE LAST LAUGH

As winter '82 settles in (June, July and August in New Zealand), a hum is in the air and planning is finalized for phase two of the highly successful Pierre Cardin campaign for Feltex, our carpet kingdom.

Other designers are considered, including Hardy Amies, Mary Quant, Christian Dior and New York designer John F. Saladino. Saladino, known as a "designer's designer," is different. He likes to mix old world ideas with the new. Staff at his New York digs is doing a fist-full of good work for several clients, including the big pop guys, Coca-Cola. His name burst onto the scene because he's seen as a progressive, rather than a traditionalist like Cardin. Burly Saladino is considered a good middleweight designer, but he doesn't have the star power of Pierre Cardin.

We have another option and it's mighty daring.

New Zealand carpet designers are in the running for the campaign. Yes, real Kiwis: bona fide ones we will pretty up with a new image and a splash of camera appeal. It might work.

In some circles it's referred to as the Hollywood treatment. Dress them daringly; give them new facial and wardrobe images. Let the finest make-up artists and hairdressers work them over, then zap them with zippy attire created by industry hot-dogs. Hey, why not?

It's a tough and controversial recommendation but John Cameron of Feltex agrees. We'll package local New Zealand designers and promote their flashy images as designers creating carpets to be included in the FELTEX INTERNATIONAL DESIGNER COLLECTION. It's obvious they'll not have the firepower of Cardin, but the concept is provocative and daring, typical of the way Murphy Truman thinks and acts: daring with a heavy dose of the usual risk.

Cardin will remain the standard bearer for the brand, as he represents the very best, the most desirable of all carpets in the world. After all, he's made enormous impact on the consumer and has great firepower, according to a marketing strategy recommendation of April 23, 1982.

For insurance, David Turner, a Feltex designer, and I will interview Saladino in New York. If he's appropriate, we might use him in the next stage to appeal to the middle-class market rather than the high-end, owned by Cardin.

Three little prigs - Marion, David and Brian

Excitement builds as three New Zealand designers are chosen to be the stars of the next television campaign. All three are plucked from the back rooms and scooted into the limelight overnight.

The reasons for the choice are clearly time spent with the company, good looks and youthful spirit. That is a decision made by the client. Soon, we meet the future stars. It makes sense to use real designers, after all, they're the brains behind a lot of what Pierre Cardin has been promoting. So, why not flush them out and paint them up the way the entertainment business package stars, then throw them in front of a camera?

Marion Newman is first. She's chosen to launch the *Vogue* collection, the trendiest shades in the colour revolution. We'll film her in New York City with the city skyline as a backdrop, flitting around, batting her eyelashes at the camera. She is the sexy bit of the threesome, with boomer-appeal for the younger middle market.

David Turner is dragged in and will be the pitchman for a new *Landscapes* collection that'll appeal to people who like the tones and textures of the English countryside. Turner is a twenty-two year veteran who has traveled the world and is plugged into trends and design change. He can speak to the masses and will be convincing, saying lines like, *"There is a hunger for colour information,"* and *"New Zealanders spend a lot of time outdoors and are greatly appreciative of the natural colors of nature. They like to bring these warm, earthy tones into their homes when carpeting (them)."* He has lots to say in a professorial way that'll up Cardin's dumb line, *"The carpets in New Zealand are made from the wood of the 'ship'!"* The obligation is easy for Turner. He loves the English countryside, so we'll film him in the lush English dales, talking about his collection. He is a natural and is turned on.

Brian Todd is next to join the team. A recent graduate of Kidderminster College (the Cambridge or Oxford of the carpet world), he is chosen to launch a Berber carpet called *Cairo Berber*. The decision about where to film him came easy: we'll send him and the crew to Cairo, to film him selling carpets in an Arab market, rambling on about texture and timeless durability. Todd will tattle on with lines like, *"Sensuality is very important in a carpet. It has to feel good. The first thing anyone does when they look at a carpet is touch it. That's sensuality."* He has the looks to carry it off.

This is no ordinary campaign: it's monumental, it's expensive and, most say, it's impossible to do in the two weeks we've allocated. Critics might say we must travel 28,855 miles (46,436 kms) around the world in record time, with absolutely no guarantee the campaign can be completed. One day, this feat could be in the Guinness Book of Records. The critics don't know us. We know it's another world first for Murphy Truman and I will be working the odyssey as a final hurrah.

The three local hot dogs do not know what is about to hit them. They'll be flung around the world, thrust in front of the cameras and will have to speak while pointing to eight, or so, three foot square carpet samples. Newman, Turner and Todd will be the new pitch team for the Feltex International Designer Collection. They're either headed for the ditch, or they'll rise to the challenge.

Rob Crabtree, the public relations manager for Feltex said, "Anyone used to media exposure (still) finds it unnerving to face a camera and speak into a microphone, so in preparation for the launch of the second collection, a practice run (or two or three or four) will have to be conducted."

Marion Newman is a real carpet designer from Kensington Carpets. She's a no-nonsense personality, married one year, who pops around New Zealand in her own plane, as she's a commercial pilot. Marion is the first we look at. Just photos, nothing more for starters. Pretty, yes, in fact downright gorgeous, but she needs a hair job, a facial scrub-up and she must learn how to move in front of the camera. A fashion consultant brought in to look at her wardrobe suggests a dishy black and white diagonally bold short-sleeve dress for her world premiere. It's all part of an exercise to make a naturally attractive girl look and move New York chic in a matter of days.

David Turner is the rugged farmer type who looks like he's been plucked from a sheep farm. The wardrobe and make up is easy: he's to look like an English country squire, wearing smart cavalry twill trousers, a trim tweedy jacket and a polo-neck sweater. The man looks good, but he doesn't speak very well. Once we fish the marbles out of his mouth and rehearse his lines a thousand times, he is on-beam.

Perhaps the easiest to work with is Brian Todd. With Hollywood good looks and trim body, he'll appeal to the younger female market. The fashion consultant decides that wearing slim white slacks and a tan coloured summer shirt this cool dude will be ready for action. The only problem with Todd is, we suspect, his jaw will stop moving when the director yells, "Action." He, too, has a schoolboy diction challenge. But the appearance is picture-perfect.

OK, we have our stars, all slightly tarnished, but better than imagined. Now we have to write the words for the campaign and organize production details for the television, radio and magazine advertising. It'll be a challenge, following in the wake of the most successful carpet launch in the world, the Pierre Cardin International Designer Collection.

David Turner, Marion Newman and Brian Todd

AIR ON A SHOE-STRING

By July 15 we're in the air, scheduled to return by August 8.

The preparation has been monumental and the budget is shoe-string tight. Ten television commercials have to be filmed for both New Zealand and Australia.

Most of the two weeks of allotted production time will be spent seven miles up.

A full crew is hired to meet in New York City, Tel Aviv and London. Locations are unknown, the weather is guesswork. All of the carpet material to appear in the commercials has been shipped ahead of the crew and will have to clear customs and be in our hands on the filming days planned for New York, Cairo and London. In all probability, we'll run into difficulties.

Only three people from the office will be at the filming from day one: me, director John Blick, from Interfilm, Wellington and his producer, the deft and detailed Norman Elder. Murphy also wants to go, but is convinced he should stay home. Blick and Elder are the team that produced the award-winning commercial for Farmbake. We like them and know how careful they are with money. Steering the project will be Nicola, a producer from Interfilm, who will remain on the phone in Wellington, 24/7, until we return. Tim Roberts, our robust account director on Feltex, will advise from afar if there are client changes.

There is a moment before any project when you either feel good, or you feel shit-scared, because you know the gamble is too big: the feeling the first astronauts must have had prior to lifting off for the moon. This one frightens all of us.

What if the star designers don't show, or arrive late for filming? What if the carpet samples don't arrive, are lost, or don't clear customs on time? What if flights are delayed or diverted due to bad weather? What about the weather on filming days? It could rain in England, or trouble could disrupt filming in Egypt. And the crew Interfilm has arranged to join us at every stop: what if they don't show, or are late, or complain about costs or the speed of production? They're unionized and could present problems, by demanding stoppages, cash payments or refusing to work late. And how will we pay for this global production? Take bags of money in various currencies, or put it in the bank, and withdraw cash as we move along or by writing cheques as needs arise – but in what currency and on what bank? Chances are good we'll be tired throughout, which will keep us in a state of senselessness. We have one shot at the gold and we have to give it a go!

New York City is our first stop and by the time I'm in the air with the director and producer it's too late to look back. It's time to open the bubbly. The movie business calls this an RDO, or a "roster day off," when there's nothing to do but kick back and relax.

After a wasted day at thirty-seven thousand feet, we land at Kennedy Airport and meet our American crew, Bob and Heather Tomei of RTG, our first team. Bob has things together; he's booked us into the fabled Plaza Hotel, facing Central Park. Carpets arrive on time and clear customs. Marion Newman arrives, looking tired but ready to get to work. At least she is there and we know with a scrub she'll look the jewel in the crown when the cameras roll.

The team scouts locations. The suggestions are the corner of Fifth Avenue and Central Park, or on the Avenue of the Americas, with the New York Marathon as a backdrop. We have a choice. No, says Elder, our producer. Too many problems, including the fact we haven't been issued permits for filming. We decide on an interior space in a hotel near the United Nations Building: the 28th floor of the UN Plaza Hotel, at 44th and 1st Avenue. Done. No weather concerns and a spectacular view of the UN and the Hudson River from the windows. Filming is set. Newman is scrubbed and wardrobed. Props are ready and the carpets, all ten of them, appear and are put on display.

The set looks great. Newman looks gorgeous and the view from the 28th floor overlooking the UN is classy. Newman's part is easy. She must move past the carpets, touch them and deliver her lines. *"New York is where fashion begins. In my VOGUE carpet range for Feltex, I've captured the best of the colour revolution...."*

Enter the first problem. A Western Union courier arrives minutes before we begin filming with a telegram saying, *"Feltex has decided that the bright - repeat bright - pink in the Vogue collection will have to be modified. Please make sure you do not highlight this carpet."* It's from Tim Roberts in Auckland. Whew, just in time!

This is explained to Newman. She'll have to skip over the pink carpet when her right hand points at the carpets on the display rack. We all know what happens next. The robot has spent two weeks rehearsing every step and gesture and every word to be spoken.

Now the director tells her to change one minor thing. She has to look at the camera, walk, gesture, speak her lines *and* skip over the pink carpet. This is a major challenge for experienced people, let alone over-rehearsed amateurs. Director Blick senses the problem and removes the pink carpet. She doesn't have to skip over it. It's that easy.

Newman gets through the scene in reasonable time, but it is tough going. Any more takes and she will heave the set out the window letting it to shower down over the United Nations Building to join the Feltex carpet already in its lobby.

The day progresses and we're buoyed by the excellent teamwork.

We return to the Plaza to find David Turner has arrived for his stopover in New York on his way to London. No problem. As the senior designer, he's here to keep an eye on progress before he heads to London to await our arrival.

While waiting in the Palm Court, drinking ice water, a two-inch thick marble tabletop breaks loose and dives to the floor. My foot is in the way. I shriek in pain, with nary a soul in sight to help. The waiter slowly, ever so slowly, comes over and snarls, "What's wrong?" I explain and he walks away. He's not interested. He never returns. The rest of the journey I'm in pain, as I continue my hobble around the world.

The other reason Turner is meeting us in New York is to accompany me to interview John F. Saladino. The meeting is scheduled for the next morning.

We arrive the next morning, and the graduate of Notre Dame and Yale School of Art and Architecture greets us and sashays through his decade-old design center.

Saladino is brisk and polished; his presentation is impressive. Coke is discussed. He points out his choice of slightly different reds for Coke bottle caps, to make them all look like the original Coke red to a world traveler. Because exterior light conditions make the colors appear different in various parts of the world like Italy, England and Egypt, different reds take this in account. Outdoors they all look like Coke red to the traveling public. I did ask what happens when viewed indoors. He didn't answer.

The Kansas City kid explains that he spent a lot of time in Rome, with fabled Italian architect Piero Sartogo. Impressive for him, I'm sure, but he left us with the impression he would not look hunky enough on camera. His mannerisms strike us as too effeminate for Kiwi taste at the time. His comments about, "…humanism from his long tradition endorsing the human scale and comfort," left me baffled. Maybe I am just too stupid to understand his complex conclusions, or maybe I smell something, so we tiptoe out and disappear without leaving a trail.

After returning to the hotel, it is time to view the *rushe*s showing Marion Newman pitching her collection. They look terrific. She's wonderful. Newman is flying high; our first designer has scored big. The film is air freighted back to Wellington, while the entourage continues on its way. That evening, we board TWA for a flight to Tel Aviv via Paris, feeling good knowing we've scored our first success with Newman.

Deep down, I know if I leave New Zealand with one outstanding commercial in my commercial reel, it'll make it easier to find employment in Toronto. This pool of commercials might be the ticket to employment. I'm praying I'll have another to add to an award-winning Farmbake commercial.

Jerusalem Cock-up

After a meal of Braised Beef Chasseur, we fall asleep. Paris is the first gas stop, then we're up again, thinking about the segment we're going to film with Brian Todd in Cairo.

People from United Studios of Israel meet us at Ben Gurion Airport in Tel Aviv. Aaron Spector, an Israeli producer, greets us and issues strict orders we're to follow. We cannot get into Egypt. They're suspicious of our motives! Therefore, the location has been changed to Jerusalem. "What the f--k," my producer screams. "That blows a hole in our plans, doesn't it?" Spector has heard it a thousand times before. He quietly says, "Don't argue. You listen, then you follow my orders." We like Spector, as he assures us, "Jerusalem is Arab-looking, and will pass for a shopping precinct in Cairo."

It's time to get off my swollen foot, take an antibiotic, which I had rustled up in New York, and relax after the ten-hour journey from New York.

Instead, we drive around Tel Aviv, looking at sights and being told what we will do the next day to complete filming. The Israelis don't ask, they tell us what to do. Finally, we arrive at the Ramada Continental Hotel on Hayarkon Street, to put our heads down for the night. And to rest my aching foot.

"*But what about Brian Todd, our star?*" I'm thinking. "*Where is he?*" Just as I'm nodding off, Todd calls to explain he's been in town for a few days and all is well. But, he doesn't have his carpet samples; they've been detained by Israeli customs, who won't release them. The package of carpet samples is deemed suspicious, he says. I'm on the phone to Aaron Spector, the big bear of a producer I'd go to war with. Spector's the fixer, the fighter, the defender and a joker. He tells me not to worry and sends me to bed after taking down the details. As filming is scheduled for the next afternoon, I'm now in a bit of a panic. After traveling half way around the world, having rehearsed his movements and timed his words, how can Todd point to *nothing* displayed in his carpet stall, while describing his bloody Berber carpets? A lesson learned in Israel is, if you have a problem, it'll only be solved by an Israeli. No one else! Stop worrying, I say to the bathroom mirror, and nod off.

Next morning, we're up with the sun and meet with the full team in the hotel lobby. But no carpets. The others don't know that I've brought carpet samples with me, just for this segment. Someone suggested we could have a problem, so I packed a slightly smaller set of carpets. Smart thinking, but they've also been retained at the airport and will be sent to the hotel for me to clear personally.

About the same time, another Telex arrives from Tim Roberts, saying, "*Feltex NZ and Australia have deleted the dark, repeat dark, green in the Cairo Berber range.*" Well, at the moment we have no carpets and we're filming in Jerusalem in a few hours. "*This is a f--king big problem,*" I'm thinking.

Spector finally arrives with two sets of carpets: one he cleared through customs; the other set is in the hotel awaiting my signature to release them. But after inspection, we have another problem. The carpet samples have grease marks on them and have had something stamped on them by the Israeli customs people, in blue ink and probably in Hebrew.

Slick Spector tumbles his belly to the dry cleaner and has them cleaned and made ready for filming within a few hours of the director saying, "Roll camera…action!" The Israelis are the world's most efficient troubleshooters.

The cavalcade of vans, with props, crew and star Brian Todd roll sixty-two kilometers down a smart dual lane highway to Jerusalem in an hour flat. Another twenty-eight kilometers and we'd be in the Dead Sea. Spector explains the Dead Sea water level has been dropping for thousands of years and will eventually dry up. Then, we'll be able to walk to Jordan. Many historic seaside towns from Biblical days are now perched on the cliffs rather than at sea level.

When we arrive in Jerusalem, a military swat-team, guns drawn, rush us through the streets to the film location. They've rented a stall from an Arab shop keeper for the day.

The props and carpets are put on display and filming begins. The sun position allows about thirty minutes to film, before the stall will fall into a shadow, making the location useless. The Israeli producer say's it'll be done in four takes. But, they don't know Todd is a novice, about to star in his first *movie!* Three carts arrive after wiggling down the cobbled steps to the location. A dozen goats, with handlers, appear, as well as two donkeys, with riders dressed in appropriate Egyptian wardrobe. Then, a dozen or so background cast members arrive; all hired for the few minutes it'll take to film this scene. By now, we've a crowd of a hundred curious onlookers, as well as police, military and the cast, surrounding Brian Todd and his makeshift stall. I can see the blood rushing from Todd's tanned face, as he gasps for air. Make-up rushes in to wet his lips. Todd is shriveling; he is drying up before our very eyes. He knows it's a daunting task.

Todd in Jerusalem

Director Blick yells the obligatory, "Roll camera...action," and the clapperboard man and camera rush into action. Filming begins. A crowd of curious gazers crush in on the set and poor Todd stalls and stammers until he gets it close enough that we can re-record his voice back in Wellington and overdub the flubs. The dark green carpet, pulled from the set at the last minute, is given to a happy shop owner in Jerusalem.

Food delivered to the set by a large, friendly Israeli production assistant is a curiosity. I'm eating what looks like a large meatball, stuffed into an ice cream cone. Spicy? Yes. Tasty? Yes. But this meat is alive: little bugs or worms are spotted on close inspection. The tension is so high that day, I dare not ask what it is, nor do I complain. I just smile and lick it down. I've other worries. My foot is starting to throb. I forgot to take my pain-killer that morning.

While awaiting the return to Tel Aviv, I'm given the August 3 issue of the *Jerusalem Post* to read. The headline said, "U.S. AND ISRAEL STILL DIFFER ON TACTICS FOR GETTING THE PLO OUT – REAGAN URGES RESTRAINT. Nothing has changed.

Prime Minister Menachem Begin doesn't like Ronald Reagan, and the Israelis, at that time, don't like the Yanks, and I sound like one. Ah ha. *"That's why I've been advised to not talk unless necessary and speak quietly."* The Israeli Defense Force (IDF) is everywhere around the cast and crew, including in front page photos in the newspaper showing Israeli soldiers walking past burned out Middle East airliners broken into bits and scattered about at Beirut International Airport.

The weather is like the inside of a toaster, reaching an uncomfortable 31 degrees C. Humidity makes clothes stick to your body like wallpaper paste. It's time to move on. It's a wrap.

To the Land of Turner

Now comes the easy part, as we're off to London to film the next segment with David Turner.

It begins with an El-Al of a trip to London. The moment I board the aircraft, I feel ill. I ate food my cultured stomach wants to reject, especially that black meat with wiggly things inside in an ice cream cone. Unfortunately, I'm seated in seat D (Zone A) on a 747, near the front of the plane. Fellow flyers spot me easily, from the right and the left, from behind and ahead, because I'm sitting in the most visible seat in the aircraft. It's the only time a sick bag with a stewardess attached arrives at my mouth, *before I think* I'm going to be sick. The black muck came flying back before we are airborne. On El Al, the aircrew knows its stuff and delivers a flawless, but very dry, flight to Heathrow.

In London, we're greeted at the Cumberland Hotel in Marble Arch by another David, our British producer. He says everything is organized. Turner has arrived. A set of carpets has been cleared by

Interfilm producer Norman Elder, so we rush to film Turner walking across Westminster Bridge, with Big Ben in the background. Neat and efficient. Then, we're whisked to the English countryside to film the exterior scenes, with Turner talking to the camera while showing his Landscapes samples.

Turner in England. The crew with Norman Elder and John Blick

The script calls for Turner to stroll through the lush green countryside near Castle Combe, in Wiltshire. The location selected by David, our producer, is visually stunning. Grey limestone cottages with mullioned windows and gabled roofs nestle in the background, a reminder of "…all things bright and beautiful, all creatures big and small, and all things wise and wonderful, the Lord God made them all." Memorable words written by Cecil Frances Alexander, 1818-1894. A babbling brook to the right is postcard-beautiful. The script calls for Turner to wave excitedly as he explains how he's been influenced by the treasures before our eyes. Then, he'll point to his collection to show how he captured these colours and textures in his timeless collection. "Beautiful, how beautiful," said client John Cameron two weeks before, back in Auckland.

No, says our British producer. David, our pommey British producer, has no appreciation for the beautiful countryside. He wants to film indoors. Is he a leftover from the Roman centurion army, which cut a swath thought this area in the fifth century, building straight roads like the Fosse Way, smack through this picturesque undulating countryside, destroying a lot of the look forever? This stuck-up wanker has no appreciation of the countryside Turner is about to describe.

How can he insist it be filmed *in the lobby* of the Manor House? There is no discussion. This is how it will be done, he screams. As much as I love British technicians and creative forces, producers will run roughshod over everyone in sight. And this is what he does. He'll film in The Manor House, or he'll pull his crew from the set.

Another telegram from Tim Roberts, in Auckland, says, *"Don't film the green carpet. It has been pulled."* I finally have a chance to put my two-pennies' worth into filming, so I shout in defiance, "Don't film the green carpet. It's been pulled!"

But the inside-outside issue is grudgingly settled; filming begins *inside* the 15th century Manor House. We've traveled half way around the world to film this lush countryside and this jerk has us bolted in the Tower of London by his resolve. No choice: we go along with his decision and, to his credit, no one notices the change in the setting when the film arrives back in Auckland. The images are magnificent. But I know they could have been even more beautiful. Much later, I discover the British producer had an agreement with the property owner that we must show the inside of his hotel. That was part of his deal! But why didn't this prat simply fess up? We'd have understood.

Turner filming indoors

The next day, we tack back to India and Indonesia via British Airways, none of which I remember as I doze off, a wounded foot in the air all the way, sans food and without refreshments.

Resting a fractured foot

The food's not very attractive, either. The "ballottine of plaice Neptune" over India turns us off. Between Perth and Melbourne, they dish-up "kidney turbigo." Finally, I perk up when they offer something familiar, "Dutch apple flan," on the final leg from Melbourne to Auckland.

I wake up with a headache and foreboding 28,855 miles later.

Production is wrapped by the middle of August and the commercial airs in September to good reviews. The final commercial is slick. The presentation is polished, but Pierre Cardin is a hard act to follow. It isn't thunder and lightning, it's a sprinkle of sweet rain.

The next step on this hugely successful campaign is to select future designers. We look inside the company once again and pluck the handsome and dashing Mark Seaward to be groomed to step onto the stage as the next dashing New Zealand designer.

Chapter 16

HOME IS WHERE THE HOUSE IS

I've made it home in time for a big celebration at Georgie Pies. New Zealanders know what Georgie Pies is; a McDonalds-like chain of family eateries that serve hot pies, of every imaginable kind, sweet to savory, accompanied by fresh cut fries, desserts and other refreshments. Such a contrast to the food that sickened me in old Jerusalem just a few days earlier.

Georgie Pies is a wonderful, fun place to visit. We have a gang of six close school friends accompanying Michelle, to celebrate her ninth birthday. When Kiwis go out to lunch, they dress up. These little pretties are no exception. They are wearing their best and behave like well-mannered children in Remuera: impeccably.

Celebrating Michelle's birthday at Georgie Pies

By October, my wife is feeling the anxiety and is spending as much time as possible with Anita Murphy, trying to ease her concerns about the future.

Our daughters prepare a birthday surprise. They bake their mother a cake. Chocolate, with nut icing, imbedded with a million chopped nuts and festooned with the letter B. Hand-painted menus are prepared and placed on the patio table. This is to be the

Baking a cake for Mother

best pauper's birthday ever and along with love and bottles of Coca-Cola, it is the sweetest.

To be cheerful with Anita and her family is especially difficult. Our once-secure future is about to drown in sorrow. We agree all occasions to celebrate will be delayed, and put in the tomorrow drawer, the exception being to have fun at birthday parties or wine tasting in the Murphy's wine cellar. Through the escalating drama, Beverley and Anita have been drawn closely together. We agree this wonderful woman deserves the most support we can give her.

ONE YEAR AFTER THE FACT

On September 23, 1982, one year after the walkout, a large party is held. The list of 121 is a VIP short list. Everyone's invited, with the exception of Lintas Sydney staff, even though it has been considered as a goodwill gesture. Clients, clients-to-be, media, suppliers, the banking community, production companies, our travel agency, recording studios and talent, right down to our Datsun dealer, are all on the guest list. They're all ready to celebrate our survival. It's an affair of the heart, with everyone professing love for each other and their dog. The band plays on. Wine flows as we continue to party even after the guests have left.

In December, with the Christmas season and good weather upon us, we head north to discover Waitangi and the enchanted Bay of Islands. We need to get away from the drama as often as we possibly can. Not talking about it, or being reminded of the outcome, is essential to our sanity. Learning more about the history of this beautiful country is an opportunity for the children and family not to be missed.

Waitangi, in 1840, was a small hamlet perched on a large hill overlooking the Hauraki Gulf and the Pacific Ocean. It's where the Maori and Europeans signed the Treaty of Waitangi, an agreement allowing both to live and work side by side and flourish. The scenery on the way up is half the joy of the trip. It'll be a once in a lifetime goodbye, maybe the best this glorious island can offer.

The Mercedes is loaded, and ready for a weekend of discovery. The journey takes us over the Nippon clip-on. The four-lane bridge from Auckland to Birkenhead was expanded from two lanes by clever Japanese engineers, who clipped-on the extra lanes. North we motor, up a wiggly road through Whangarei and hamlets like Paihia and finally up the hill to Waitangi. The roads are good. Traveling up Highway 1 or Highway 12, we can see the Pacific Ocean on the right and the Tasman Sea on the left. East and west are separated by a big finger of land that points straight north. The view is completely different in each direction. The Maoris say it's the difference between the savage male and the gentle female.

The west coast, pounded by the Tasman, is the male side. It has an endless coast line of dark sand interrupted by big harbors fronting towns like Manukau, Kaipara, and Hokianga, where treacherous sand bars act like lighthouses.

The eastern female side is gentle, with sheltered bays, peninsulas, islands and alluring white sand stretching to the big frothy Pacific.

The view is spectacular no matter which way we turn. Up hills, down valleys, through deserted gold towns, swinging right, then dropping down to the waterline to navigate over tiny bridges, it is spectacular. The view is sheer rolling beauty with lush greens, exotic pines, bright yellows, rock pillars reaching from sea-bed to the sky, patches of jasmine covering gentle hills. Soft ochres and incandescent blues excite the film in my camera, making it a struggle to drive in a straight line. When we finally pull into the THC motel in tiny Waitangi, we're ready to cark out.

The next day, we visit Treaty House at Waitangi and Whare Rununga. Then we tour the Shipwreck museum where they've reconstructed a sugar barge, like the mighty wooden squeaker in the popular television series, The Onedin Line.

Finally, we end our brief vacation on the Mount Cook Lines ship the Tiger Lilly, watching marine life in the wild. It doesn't disappoint us, particularly the sea turbulence, as Nicole's green face attests. In fact, it's scary for all of us. The return journey doesn't disappoint either, as we keep to the female side of the finger of land Kiwis call the winterless north.

In November, Marshall Taylor announces that Caxton has awarded the Treasures baby products account to the agency. This is a major piece of new business. With our female writer in place, it seems to be her big challenge. We'll begin work in January 1983. Caxton has a solid track record, selling more than four million packets of disposable nappies a year. Within hours, we're planning a radio and newspaper ad campaign to appear in the New Year.

We needed this win, as we're getting nervous about making a profit.

Snow is not a four-letter word

Christmas comes and goes, with the usual twig for a Christmas tree and the sizzle of warm rays melting images of traditional cheer. We know by now one of the reasons we came south has become one of the reasons to go home: snow and ice and the extreme seasons. We miss them and, no matter what is said, having family and friends so far away makes the heart heavy. I once said *snow* is a four-letter word. Not any more!

Oh, how the family pined for something familiar, despite the privileges, despite the good life, the Mercedes, the pool, the lemon groves, and the outdoor life. Yes, we cried dry tears in the dark shadows for the little things we missed. Canada has become a photo album of illusions. The further you are from them, the more beautiful they become.

But the frustration for me is there's no career prospect to look forward to going home. No matter which way we point, we'll lose.

January 1983 arrives and summer waves from the skies.

It's time to plan for the inevitable return to Canada in eight months.

The house in Toronto has been rented to another family, so we believe things will remain stable. We have to be home by September, to allow the children to return to school at the normal time and for me to find employment in a depressed market.

Money to pay for repairs to the house and to top-up lower rental fees have been flying to Canada every month since the problem was recognized. We've drained our limited resources and exhausted our enthusiasm.

The end is near

It's now time to sell my shares in the company, but at a terrible cost. Other problems have surfaced that further complicate matters.

David and Anita are clearly having marital problems. Although most are aware of the problem, we try to keep it underground.

Unfortunately, it doesn't take long for the shipwreck to appear for all to see. David has moved out of his family home and rented a small flat in town.

Looking back, his problem probably began with the decision to hire a *female* writer. Murphy, for all the right reasons, is taking a special interest in her welfare. It isn't the fact she's Australian or a writer; it's that she's attractive and single and needed. The affair, or relationship, whatever it is, affects his marriage and the company, but I don't think he is aware of the extent of the emotional damage. We are because we've been talking to Anita. He is feeling pressure from the breakaway to form the new agency, the financial noose being tightened by Lintas, and the difficulty of running a successful company. Financial problems continue to bog the agency down, even with the intrepid David Downham running the finances of the company. We are as close to being a fatality as you can get. Undoubtedly, we both have emotional turmoil to contend with.

Hiring the wrong person is a concern for any company. I believe we hired the wrong person in a hurry, at the wrong time, for the wrong reason. She is given an opportunity and is not to be faulted for jumping at the job offer.

It takes very little to damage the delicate trust holding a temperamental group of people, *and their wives*, together. Therefore, it surprised no one when the relationship surged to the surface and damaged our relationship. Nothing was planned. It just happened because Murphy is vulnerable. The pot is boiling with a mixture of loneliness, despair and fear of financial ruin, aggravated by alcohol and primitive instincts.

About this time, I believe Murphy lost his way. The problems related to the breakaway upset his balance and Murphy crawled inside himself, alone in grief. The Murphy of old, the bright breezy marketing poet with the schoolboy grin and an answer to every challenge is weathered. The pummeling has taken a toll. Eyes are puffy, and he's alone in thought most of the time. In my view, his management style changed. He now runs the operation with tough love. He has every right to do so, given that he and his wife finance the venture and therefore take all of the risks. But it's obvious that his partner, dear Anita, is probably not involved in any business decisions and she needs help too.

As turmoil slips into the closet, work issues scurry to the surface and assignments carry on, including the launch of another new product phenomenon called crisp bread, an air-filled slice of a toast-like cracker that doesn't crumble and make a mess when you bite into it. Quite clever, but a little tasteless.

I slowly lose interest in the business. My enthusiasm is ebbing. I must look to my future in Canada. The agency is morphing into a new form. The new agency team tackles the challenge to name and package the product, to the delight of the Aulsebrooks team. The new name is Cruskits, a combination of the word crunchy and the word biscuit.

The launch is planned for the fall of 1983, but I must return to Canada by September. It is clear I'll not be around to develop this major product launch. Therefore, it's time to throw the big challenge to our new writer and let her deal with it without advice from me. Murphy concurs and welcomes the opportunity to work more closely with her. It's a big opportunity for her to demonstrate her talent.

Although my team developed the name, positioning and packaging, the bigger task of writing a creative strategy and a television campaign is left to the new team. My lifeless spirit is already rowing away from the crippled ship.

Soon, Cruskits has a new positioning line. *"Cruskits, the all crunch, no crumble (a good selling feature), wheat slice."* The packaging copy reads, *"Imagine a totally new taste sensation. It's crisp and light with lots of crunch. But when you cut or bite into it, no crumble."*

The television campaign, based on the movie, *Murder on the Orient Express*, appears in the fall and is sensational. It's colossal, a mega-buck production. True to form, Murphy is willing to gamble. He is coming back strong. I am proud of the effort, as the end result is a riveting television commercial.

Morris 1100 "clunker"

In mid-summer, Beverley needs a bit more mobility, and buys an old, used Morris 1100, a baby blue clunker that cost $2,000. Hopefully, it'll last a few months, then we can sell it. But problems begin the day she drives it home. After stopping in the driveway, it dies, and it will not start. The old clunker has to be towed by Takapuna Haulage to a garage and repaired for an additional $210, or 10% of what we've just paid for the car. But when it's repaired, she's mobile and we get on top of personal stuff and keep our daughters on the move.

Chapter 17

BAILING OUT - SELLING UP

On March 15, 1983, I officially resign, to let the company find footing without damaging any part of a well-oiled, but temporarily bruised, machine. When they replace my contribution, the agency will bounce back and be better than ever. It's also possible the new writing talent from Australia will fill the writing void admirably. Bravely stated, but the financial settlement that could destroy the agency still faces us.

I must now sell my shares in the company to build my financial war chest for the return trip to home in Canada.

Downham asks me to value my shares and get back to the company. Although I'd committed to buying 22% of the company shares, I've only paid for 11% and still believe I owe the company money. Now, a new battle is underway, with both sides hiring advisors to try to sort out the mess. It is expensive, but necessary. Good will is out of place when it comes to money.

Goliath is not aware of the undercurrent of problems cutting into the roots of our stability. With all the other problems we're facing, selling my shares seems a trivial issue. Suddenly, all hell breaks loose, as the big problem facing us becomes a lot clearer.

THE FINAL BLOW

On March 18, a letter from the Lintas lawyer to our lawyer delivered the impending punch to the gut that had been keeping us awake in the dark of night.

Lintas demands a certain amount of money to settle losses in what it refers to as a *prayer for relief, for the alleged loss it has suffered*.

Mitigation expenses, or the amount of staff time Bruce Harris claimed is needed in clearing up the mess are big. He alone has recorded a claim of $20,000. When we add on seven others involved in sorting out the mess, Flint, Moxey, Webley, O'Sullivan, Spence, Scott and Gosling, it comes to a grand total of $28,548. This amount is for time charges only I'm told, from September 22 to the end of 1981.

Airfares, cabs, accommodation, car hires and miscellaneous costs total another $33,456.

The big charge of $162,000 is for "loss of opportunities to retain profitable connections." Or, we have an option to pay $81,031 for loss of profit.

The grand total is $224,004. In plain English, that's the amount Murphy and I have to fork over to settle this part of the case.

Phew, the punch from Goliath lands. It's time for a counter-attack.

Correspondence from our lawyer dated March 18 asks Downham for a comment on the demands. He summarizes it in a light-hearted way *"Good grief, it looks as though Lintas made a profit out of the whole affair! Doug, what are the chances of David and Richard being reimbursed by Lintas?"*

The claims suggest they had either been living like fat cats, or had been padding everything to include costs beyond working on this case. Some suggest Harris might have been in Auckland working on other business, but it's mere speculation.

In addition, Lintas had business income from September 1981 to December 1981, since Aulsebrooks and Feltex honoured their termination agreements and paid Lintas *for ongoing work for the three last months including media commission*. This income should have been deducted from their demands. There is also suspicion some other staff members might have been in Auckland on other business. No documentation to support the claims is volunteered.

The continued lashing had been expected, but there was a fist of steel balls behind each punch, a brutal attempt for a knockout blow. "We're not going to be intimidated, however. The tougher they get, the more determined we will become," we said. Here we are, despite personal problems, and unforeseen events, sticking together to defend ourselves from the onslaught, because we have to keep our business viable. The only option is battling back, asking for reconsideration of demands that we know are excessive and designed to drive us out of business as quickly as possible.

The Harris charm is now a death stalk. So we punch back like drunken sailors, fighting for our lives, and wait.

On the way home that evening, I gas up and collect another Smurf. This time, it's Baker Smurf. My daughters, "Pumpkin" and "Peanut" (their nicknames) will be thrilled as they don't have Baker. But the newest Smurf did suggest, when I read my blue tealeaves, that Lintas is baking a cake and going to eat it, too.

I am still looking for Convict Smurf, as he seems appropriate for what lies ahead. By now, shadows frighten me. Where am I going to find more than $100,000 to settle my share of the lawsuit?

A goodbye Canadian birthday party

May creeps up, and we're ready to celebrate another birthday. This is Nicole's eighth and it's a big one, her last in New Zealand. I know where her heart is, even though she was born in Guildford, England and has spent no more than four years in Canada. Deep down she's Canadian and is proud of it, even though she might not yet understand why.

To celebrate, fourteen of her Corran friends and neighbourhood children have been invited to mark the occasion. But there is a twist. Her friends are to dress in Canadian style. How will they know what that means? Well, mums know best. They step in and make special red and white dresses. Most look like the Canadian flag. All the girls' mums make hats, with large, protruding gold maple leaves. It's a bewildering array of nationalism as the little darlings from so far away give Nicole her best birthday ever.

Allison, a classmate from Corran, is chosen as the best dressed. Dear little red-haired, freckled, pretty Allison seemed sad that day. The wrap-up for the party is the lighting of fireworks and the downing of a foot long birthday cake that almost looked like the Canadian flag.

By April, my tax advisor suggests a strategy for selling my shares and indicates an amount I should sell them for.

I paid $5,500 to purchase 11,000 shares. I still owe the company another $5,500 for the additional 11,000 shares I agreed to buy. My response is to ask for $110,000 for the 22% I planned to buy, then repay the company the $5,500 owed on 11,000 shares. I am advised this is a fair amount. At the time, I believe it's fair. Basic math, for sure. I assume that during more than two years of doing business, the share value should have increased considerably from the original cost of 50 cents. But, in hindsight, I had forgotten a golden rule.

I wait for a response from Downham, who is charged with resolving the messy issue.

Westpac Towers Ahead

With chaos and uncertainty all around, the next step is familiar.

A business proposal submitted to Westpac Bank, requesting a further extension of credit, is approved.

The agency bravado, the sheer aggression by leadership and the need for more space led us to the conclusion that we must move to something "smart" and progressive to reflect Murphy's determination and spirit. Before long, and after lengthy negotiation with the Westpac landlord, Murphy Truman agrees on a full four-floor slice of a new seven-storey tower. The Westpac building is already under construction at 100 Symonds Street. A gutsy move for sure, it's designed to push our image up to the heavens despite the enormous problems.

A party is held during construction, after which the final colour scheme of coral and polished chrome is chosen. The new premises will be smart: high fashion, a place where clients and staff can relax in good company.

Celebrating a new head office

On May 1, 1983, a lavish party is held. Clients are invited, as well as the media, staff and their spouses. The invitation said, *"The atmosphere of this agency-warming will be distinctly relaxed. The dress – Sunday Casual, to suit the time of day. Breakfast will be served at 9 A.M. prior to David Murphy's official opening ceremony at 10 A.M. To tempt your palate we offer the following delicacies available for consumption on the day."*

The smart new image might just buy the agency out of trouble; it's been done before and will be done again in the ad biz.

The delicacies are named after clients. "Brice" pudding is named after one of our clients, Mr. Brice. Amusing, yes, but it's also an opportunity for clients to see the work we do for other clients. Clients are also invited to mingle and talk with staff. Many staff members had not met with customers socially in the past. A dangerous precedent because staff after a few drinks might make uncomfortable comments, but it works out well.

Driving into the front parking lot, clients can't miss twelve "reserved for Murphy Truman" signs stenciled on the pavement, which give everyone a lift. The eight shiny Grey Datsuns, a Mercedes and a Jag look smart sitting in slots now ready to be occupied by clients.

On the surface, everything seemed wonderful, but in reality the glue had come unstuck, for the obvious reasons. My unexpected need to return home to Canada has left the Murphys exposed and alone. Murphy's difficulty at home, with a separation from his wife masked to a degree, shows on his face. We don't know whether the separation can be resolved. And, I have to find employment when I return to Toronto. Finally, the Lintas lawsuit charging us with costs of more than $100,000 each cannot be met, even though it is demanded. A delay is the only option.

Our financial situation is such that the Murphy Truman agency will make it to the end of 1983. The mountain of debt has probably grown, but to what level I do not know, as I've had little involvement in the finances of the agency recently. I have every right to look at the books, but I don't think it'll reveal what I need to know. The mumbo-jumbo of finance is not understood, but should have been, as without it you cannot lead from the front. What will happen in the future? Can the agency get out of this mess? Is MTA headed toward a profitable future? I do not have answers. Even if I looked at the books it would reveal little.

My wife is suffering from severe anxiety, knowing the road ahead is blocked by a serious recession in Canada and the probable loss of our house in West Hill. We are sure that Lintas is not going to stop: it has the billions needed to thump out the little guys, the sooner the better. We know we cannot hide.

The same weekend, New Zealand has honored visitors who will distract us and break the tension momentarily.

A Princess calls

Princess Diana, Prince Charles and baby William visit Auckland, in time to lift our spirits.

After a welcome by Mr. and Mrs. Kaye, the Mayor and Mayoress, the Royals enjoy mixing with Kiwis. Charles plays polo at Clevedon, while Diana visits with school children, doing what she does best, talking to them. Our daughters Michelle and Nicole are in the crowd with their class mates and teachers, but never manage to get too close.

The Royals rush to important sites like the Cenotaph, One Tree Hill, a sailing regatta and Government House. Diana is stunning, such a blessing for the Royals to have such a beautiful future Queen. When she greets Parnell school children at Eden Park, Princess Diana is wearing a simple green dress; her head is crowned by a snugly fitted white hat, with feathers cascading down her back. Diana is a treasure never to be lost to this adoring nation. Fresh-faced Diana is

no more than a child amidst the celebration.

Charles is handsomely dressed and carries himself with dignity, whether wearing Air Force blues or formal dress. With the swagger of James Bond, and youthful film star, he's definitely a future king. Little Prince William is simply an adorable infant. Kiwis watch, smitten, in a love trance, believing they will soon lead our commonwealth of nations.

We follow most of the tour on television, including watching them brave Auckland's rainy days. Every step of the tour is an obsession, as we whisper *"oohs and aaahs"* from the comfort of our family room couch, surrounded by kittens, Smurfs and our children.

ANITA'S GIFT

Clients are fine; business is good. But I still toss and turn in the dark. The company is ensconced in delicious new premises and the staff is in good spirits. At the moment, Lintas anger doesn't reach the shop floor.

It's time to sell my shares, my part ownership of the company, and depart with dignity and honour, and hopefully have friends to count on in the future.

First a lesson is learned that I shall not forget.

If a partner sells out, the share value does NOT go up, it goes down.

The original share value was 50 cents. The departure of a key partner means the most it will be worth is no more than half the original value, or 25 cents.

I have walked into a can of embarrassing worms and agree the company should not pay the price I've asked, of nearly $110,000. How ludicrous. In fact, I will be lucky if I get back my investment of

$5,500. But I must have a financial settlement to help pay for the return home and to begin rebuilding shattered finances.

The Murphy Truman partners have a decision to make.

The final decision is a combination of Downham's recommendation, the partners' agreement and Murphy's acceptance. I wait.

In the end, the Murphy Truman agency is generous.

They agree to airfares of nearly $4,000 for the family and an additional $7,000 to ship household furnishings back to Canada. This is remarkable, considering the dilemma I left behind. We will pay to fly our three prized breeding cats back to Canada. The generosity of the company is overwhelming, but I still have the outstanding issue of selling my shares, *which means someone has to buy them*. But there are no takers.

At the same time, our family of Smurfs suffers the most catastrophic blow of all. The Smurfs are now a prized collection my daughters want to take back to Canada. They believe it'll excite their school chums and neighbourhood friends. By now, they have each collected over seventy little blue friends. They clean them every day and display them on shelves in their bedrooms. They have become close friends. Late in the evening, when they're supposed to be asleep, I hear them whispering to Baby Smurf, or Smurfette, or Papa Smurf about their trials and tribulations at school. They don't know I'm listening.

They arranged a goodbye party for as many of their friends as we can pack into our house one day after school. They party most of the day and the children leave by early evening. When they return to their bedrooms, however, they're shocked and horrified.

Someone has cut off the Smurfs' legs, as if a madman with a chainsaw has de-legged one hundred and forty of their little friends. We know they cuddle Baby Smurf, Slouchy, Snappy, Painter, Slouchy, Snappy, Farmer, Dreamy, Harmony, with his trumpet, Brainy, Clumsy, pretty little Smurfette and even King Smurf and have a little talk with each of them. They never chat to Lazy Smurf, because he is always asleep. Papa, the only Smurf who wears red, is the best listener. The Smurfs represent a little civilization of a different kind. How can we explain the disaster that struck their little blue friends? We never discover who did it or why. The tears don't dry up for some time.

The issue of the sale of my shares still haunts me, as we need the money to survive and resettle. A phone call, out of the blue, has us in a flood of tears. Anita Murphy, David's wife, calls to say she's decided to buy the shares from us *personally,* to see us on our way. She will give us cash to help us through our difficulties. Tears flow, tears of joy and tears of love for this wonderful woman.

"*All the beautiful sentiments in the world, weigh less than a single lovely action.*" (Ib.) We are free at last. After nearly three years of struggle and love, the pain of loss, we are flooded by a cornucopia of emotions ranging from love and joy to sadness, remorse and guilt.

The hero of the decade is Anita Murphy. One day we will thank her again.

Murphy Truman goes international

But this is not the end of Murphy Truman as I know it.

The brilliant chameleon that Murphy is, has cranked up the engine and he's back to dreaming big, as only David Murphy can. He decides to open an office in Australia, the first of a number of international offices we dreamed about just a few months back. And he is determined.

The loss of a partner allows him to breathe deeply, focus on something new and move on. Can he afford it? Probably not, but it'll be done.

If we can pay the damages lawsuit, both of us know the final hurdle will be overcome and we can really celebrate victory.

Murphy accepts that our dream of being partners is over, but the dream of the Murphy Truman agency isn't.

His wife and family might have paid the ultimate price at the time. We pray they will reach out to each other in the months ahead.

I've been torpedoed by a depression in Canada in 1983, and maybe deep down I've been spurred on by an emerging excitement about the future. Perhaps I realize that I'm Canadian and *going home* for good, after years of living in Africa, London, Paris, Brussels and Auckland.

So the name Murphy Truman marches into Australia to take on the multi-nationals, like Lintas, that so brutalized a small enterprising New Zealand agency.

Murphy's talent and ego have exceeded his desire to manage domestic growth, so he goes international. SYDNEY WELCOMES MURPHY TRUMAN. Australia? It's merely the beginning.

I let go. I'm now heading northeast. I'm out of the loop. Settlement of the lawsuit is not finalized while I'm in Auckland. It's been delayed and will follow me to Canada.

Chapter 17

WE'RE GOING, WE'RE GONE

On a quiet Auckland Sunday, we depart for home with a sense of pride in achievement. We take the last breath of daphne, honeysuckle and sweet rose that soften the quilt of Pacific air and head to the airport.

On August 14, 1983, the family looks back as Air Pacific 443 scoots through the pretty blue sky to Fiji. It's a little bewildering. We left behind a life that was *nearly* perfect. One day, the children will know the details of the drama that has been played out and maybe understand why it ended the way it did.

In Fiji, we board a CP Air DC 10 that hurls us through the black Pacific night to Hawaii. The journey is uncomfortable and the first sign of reality: we're flying nearly cargo class. Once in Hawaii, the family decides to thank Anita. It's time to live it up. Royal Canadian Class beckons, so we move to the front of the Empress of Rome jetliner. We owe our future to dear Anita Murphy. Once on board we whisper, *"This is the way to go,"* to the children as the door to another chapter is gently closed. We've tasted the good life and liked it. The best of New Zealand's breeding cats follow us in a few weeks, to a different playground in the snow. The legless Smurfs came home with us, too. Casualties from happier times, that have felt pain, too.

Between Honolulu and Toronto, my daughters have a special surprise. They open a brown sandwich bag, to show us a collection of new Smurfs, given to them by their school friends, just before they left New Zealand.

Not all of them, but most of them have joined us on the journey home. And they are whole as Smurfs are intended to be. Their friends collected as many as they could, just for them. That is a special celebration somewhere over the blue Pacific.

This is the kind-hearted Kiwi we left behind and will always miss.

New Zealand is a magnificent land filled with wonderful people that gave us a chance to learn and an opportunity to grow, and offered a lifestyle that is, perhaps, the way life is supposed to be.

All together again, seven miles up

Chapter 18

LOSERS AND WINNERS

There were losers for sure, but most of the key characters in this tale are winners. Lessons were learned, by many individuals, but primarily by the multi-national companies that fell asleep at the wheel of common sense and good governance.

Most summaries in the narrative are *opinions* expressed by the players in this book. That is what this story is all about: opinions, notably mine. After all, the world is ruled by opinion. Some say opinions are a private matter. But then, *"The world is governed by opinion, so I have a right to stake my claim, even if I tend to treat all opinions as principles."* A lovely line borrowed from Herbert Agar. Sir Robert Peel wrapped a ribbon around opinion when he said, *"Public opinion is a compound of folly, weakness, prejudice, wrong feeling, right feelings, obstinacy and newspaper paragraphs."*

But in the end, the public has an interest in judgements only and they soon follow.

THE LOSERS?

David Murphy probably lost a considerable amount of cash. His marriage and family life might also have been short-term victims. But under his stewardship, Murphy Truman Advertising did continue to operate for a while, allowing him to recoup some losses. The company was sold to a New Zealand agency on July 31, 1984, then subsequently sold to Saatchi and Saatchi in May of 1985, according to Mike Howard. The amount it is sold for and the eventual income derived from the sale remain a mystery. But the account services people and the media department follow Murphy to Saatchi and Saatchi, Auckland when the company is purchased.

Two veterans who didn't follow the gang to Saatchi were David Russell and the man that did so much to keep Murphy Truman afloat and sane, the charming and lovable rascal, David Downham.

One of the senior men, Mike Howard said, "In the end Murph lost – and lost plenty. I would say that Murph was the most incredible adman I ever worked with – creative, charismatic, vibrant, energetic but also a polarizer. Because he just streeted people, he paid a huge price."

For a man who simply wanted to resign and set up his own agency, this genious and passionate adman paid too big a price. It is so unfair.

Murphy, the talented giant from the little islands might well agree. *"My candle burns at both ends; it will not last the night; but, ah, my foes, and oh, my friends – it gives lovely light!"* Thank you, Edna St. Vincent Millay for this fitting tribute.

I, **Donald Richard Truman,** lost short-term cash due to the recession in Canada. I lost my home to the ravages of the recession and endured the cost of rebuilding the family's fortunes, after a failed attempt at agency building so far from home. In the end, Lintas stopped chasing me for a settlement. Lawyers could not be paid to continue my defense in New Zealand. Therefore, everything drifted away.

Murphy chased me to help settle. I was tracked down while working at J. Walter Thompson. On September 11, 1984, J. Walter Thompson in Toronto received the first fax: *"Please advise urgently whether you have a Donald Richard Truman working at your agency. If so, please advise him that he must contact me urgently, to his own advantage. If not, please advise whether you know his whereabouts."*

November 16, a final telex from David Murphy sent to me while I was filming a Midas commercial in Hollywood, stated, *"Michael Curtis at Buddle Weir waiting your instructions. Suggest you call him very urgently to obtain adjournment. Delay could be most expensive for you."*

I responded to Mr. Johnson, my ex-legal counsel in Auckland, advising that I was bankrupt. During this period, I discovered my name and career were damaged by international reporting and I was encouraged to sue Lintas and David Ogilvy at a future date. At the time, the worldwide book by advertising guru Ogilvy, *OGILVY ON*

ADVERTISING is being widely read and some knew that David and I were the "two" referred to in his book.

The court case against us is delayed past April 1985, with no fixed date for settlement. By April 15, 1985, I wrote directly to the judge and pleaded my case including the damage done by David Ogilvy's "untrue and unsubstantiated" comments reported in his best-selling book.

At the time, I borrowed a line by William Bradford that said, *"One small candle may light a thousand."* I believe I did light one small candle.

Lintas, in my opinion lost much, but the industry gained by the experience.

Why do I believe Lintas lost?

They did not keep an eye on small market offices. As long as small markets contribute to the bottom line, those at the top appear to be disinterested. Instead they focus on new business, enjoyment by their legless leaders and squeaks from shareholders.

Lintas did not develop potential in the ranks if the individuals were located in small markets. Murphy is a fine example.

If David Murphy had worked in London or New York or, indeed, Canada he would have been spotted as a rising star, and groomed. He had everything agencies are looking for today and clients attest to his talents years later. Bruce Harris hinted that he might have done things without considering the consequences. This book certainly suggests the judgement is partly wrong.

Finally, Lintas doesn't understand local sensibilities. Why rush Australians in to solve a Kiwi mess, which is a "local" issue.

In the end of this trial, it is Kiwis vs. the annoying Australians. And Kiwis won. David has clobbered Goliath, on this account alone.

<u>And, Murphy Truman won all of the accounts that left Lintas for the breakaway group. Lintas lost **all** of the accounts. Why?</u>

Lintas was good to me and was generous, but after this experience I believe the roots and branches of the operation were desperately in need of a root-and-branch change. That is my opinion.

Bruce Harris did a wonderful job attempting to rebuild, but I do not believe he had thought details through as thoroughly as he might have in hind-sight.

At the first sign of trouble, he should have talked first and not built adversarial walls. He could have talked with me. After all, I was the only legal-director in the Auckland office. They didn't.

Instead, there is sudden hostility and defiance, never wanting to understand "why" it has happened.

In my opinion it was a consensual reaction by senior staff, operational staff and clients. Everything just fell into our hands. *Lintas unintentionally forced them all away.*

THE WINNERS?

David Murphy, perhaps with partners, ended up with an agency he passed on to Saatchi and Saatchi, one of the most successful new-wave agency groups.

The Murphy Truman agency headed by Murphy, won and *kept all clients* that followed him from Lintas with the exception of one, and *all of the staff* with the exception of an easily replaced writer. That is an unimaginable victory for the little man.

Murphy deserves credit for controlling a losing situation in stormy seas and for turning it into a positive and dynamic movement. He also demonstrated an enormous talent that was never fully appreciated by Lintas. If anything he won by demonstration.

Murphy also raised the standards of advertising and marketing excellence in New Zealand, perhaps unduplicated. He will be remembered by many as an innovator and a brave individual in a hostile industry.

The last I heard of David after he left the advertising business, he was active in desktop publishing in Auckland, then moved back to London, then moved to Gisborne as rumour would have it, but always remained close to the industry he loved. That's the last I know of him, despite valiant efforts to track down every D. J. Murphy in New Zealand.

What happened to **D. Richard Truman?**

After returning to Canada, I enjoyed a successful career with J. Walter Thompson in Toronto. I became a vice-president and was awarded the cherished VP tie. My immediate supervisor at J. Walter Thompson, Norman Rigg, Sr. VP, rated my performance as "outstanding" and said, *"While it is difficult to single out one individual when it is usually an entire team which contributes to an 'outstanding' score,*

I would like to make special mention of Richard Truman. Richard's contributions, high level and enthusiasm, and general interest in our business have earned the respect of the marketing groups. His leadership of the creative team has contributed significantly to this outstanding rating, 4.5 out of 5."

Despite the recession, I found employment rather quickly, because the work I'd developed for New Zealand clients demonstrated my understanding of business. Everything I learned in New Zealand was applied and is the reason for my later success.

J. Walter Thompson is still regarded as the greatest teacher and, undoubtedly, one of the finest "thinking" agencies on the planet.

In New Zealand, I traveled 86,565 miles, around the globe three times in 943 days, perfecting my craft and expanding horizons that would allow me to invest in future success. My children were privileged to travel 57,710 miles before the age of 10, all the while learning about other cultures and seeing rare global beauty.

But I always remember the freedom and independence of doing my own thing in New Zealand: the exhilaration of doing original advertising and not being forced to use material from New York, or London.

Our Canadian culture continues to be usurped by foreign advertising aired to the cheers of fat cats in New York and London. There is no regard for the culture of smaller societies.

After three years, I left J. Walter Thompson, to follow what I'd learned and practiced in New Zealand. It was a cathartic moment; business skills and creative freedom developed in New Zealand were at the heart of my newfound Canadian company, Campaign House Worldwide.

Within a few years, the company had partners around the world and championed successful clients for 14 years. Meetings were held with independent partners in Johannesburg, London, Chicago, Oslo, Paris and India. The list went on and proved that small independents can do well without intrusion by multi-national advertising agencies. We fought the same battles as the multi-nationals and we won. Before retirement, I sold the agency to a division of a European-headed consortium called Cordiant, once brothers with Saatchi and Saatchi. They in turn sold the agency to Ogilvy, a division of WPP. Murphy Truman is the reason I succeeded as an independent in this combative business.

The multi-nationals: They learned lessons and tightened the rules of engagement worldwide. Employees are now warned not to try breaking away or they'll be slapped in irons, and the key will be tossed away. So, it probably slowed the exodus of individuals intent on resigning and starting new ventures.

At the end of the day, **Lintas** won, too, satisfied with the results of the court case, according to Bruce Harris. The Auckland office overcame the loss because of the efforts of the charming and engaging Max Gosling, who was appointed managing director of SSC&B Lintas New Zealand shortly after the bust-up.

Gosling did a fine job rebuilding the Auckland office to full strength with billings over $7 million. Not a bad result, after a yearlong effort. In fact, the Lintas agency appeared to be almost back to norm until it too was sold.

Nine times out of ten in advertising, as in life, there is no truth to be discovered. There is only error to be exposed.

For my friends in New Zealand, just think what Lintas Auckland could have been, had someone listened many years ago.

Chapter 20

In Summary

The judgement by the court is that we failed in our fiduciary duty, or the legal relationship between two or more parties was broken. According to law, the fiduciary, or "Murphy and Truman" is expected to be extremely loyal to the person to whom they owe the duty (Lintas) and we must not put our personal interests before the duty, and must not profit from our position as a fiduciary, unless the principal (Lintas) consents. Therefore, the fiduciary relationship is highlighted by good faith, loyalty and trust.

The saga however, in my view, is the result of a mistake. The walkout was not a master plan executed by brilliant strategists, it just looked that way. Like dominos, everything fell into our laps because of deep-rooted respect. The staff members liked each other and enjoyed working together. Clients got what was expected - results, from an exceptional ad agency under the exceptional leadership of David Murphy and his team.

Good clients reserve the highest accolades for marketing and advertising people who solve problems and get results - we did!

In 1983, reading David Ogilvy's *"OGILVY ON ADVERTISING,"* a read recommended by a friend at J Walter Thompson, I reached page 62, and was spitting nails.

How dare he say, *"...In 1981 an agency in New Zealand took successful action against its former Managing Director and Creative Director who had walked out with 17 members of the staff and nine accounts. Gentle reader, you have been warned."*?

"You have been warned," and *"successful action..."* What does that

mean? Years later, these words stimulated me into writing this book. **We had won the battle… just.**

Oh, how quickly the multinational ad agencies bury a loss in quicksand and call it a victory. Perhaps the little man has no voice, after all.

In summary, *justice is relatively easy to bear; what stings most is injustice.*

The end

A Special Tribute

During the intervening years, we have lost special friends. Murphy Truman lost two of its stalwart leaders and members of the inner-five management team.

David Downham gave so much loyalty and goodwill, dedicating every ounce of energy to building the offices of both Lintas Auckland and Murphy Truman. Unfortunately, he was in a serious car accident while I was still in New Zealand.

After the sale of Murphy Truman, he was no longer needed and turned his energies to developing a company he founded, called, "Feets of Clay," creating lovable clay items for the home.

According to ex-partner David Russell, the combination of the accident and other pressures were too much to bear. He took his own life shortly thereafter. We all miss this gentle man and will always remember him fondly for his joyful spirit and the laughter he generated while he was with us.

Tim Roberts was one of our account services directors at Murphy Truman. Tim was the big burly guy who loved life; he made us laugh, made us cry, challenged us and comforted us. Tim, with the booming voice that could be heard a block away, was the soul who kept in touch with us half a globe away during the filming of the Feltex commercials. Tim and his wife Diana and family returned to her home town of Gisborne to finally settle.

Dear Timmy is no longer with us. We miss him dearly.

Antagonists, too, are men to be admired and certainly one of the best was actively involved in the Lintas Auckland and Murphy

Truman file. **Jean-Francoise Lacour** had a great career with Lintas and was the guiding light that traveled the world, putting out fires, inspiring the regions and leading his troops in a highly combative industry. In mid 1982, he was summoned to London HQ to be told he would replace charismatic Philipe Charmet as chairman of the biggest Lintas office in Europe, nestled in the prestigious and powerful Paris office on the Seine. He had reached the pinnacle of success as the head of Europe's biggest advertising group, but didn't take the big chair.

Lacour, the brilliant and energetic Frenchman, had almost arrived. Lacour's eye problem proved to be a symptom of a developing brain tumor which was finally diagnosed in 1983 and was to lead to an untimely death. We will never know whether it contributed to his behaviour during the crises. His passing kept him from the big chair.

About The Author

D. Richard Truman was born in the steel city of Hamilton, Ontario, Canada and began writing as an advertising copywriter in Toronto.

During his forty-five year career, he worked with major international advertising agencies in North America, Europe, Africa and Australasia.

After twenty-five years working in the international market, he returned home. A few years after returning to Toronto, he set up his own company, Campaign House, which emerged as the Canadian nucleus of a worldwide group of "boutique" agencies, a considerable achievement in a savagely competitive industry dominated by American and British mega-agencies.

Nearing retirement, Truman sold Campaign House Worldwide to Bates, part of the Cordiant Group, plc of London, England.

Richard has been listed in Who's Who in Canada for the past eight years. After retirement, Richard and his British-born wife Beverley moved to Kitchener, Ontario, Canada.

Richard is the father of two daughters, Michelle Stafford and Nicole Hall and has four grandchildren: Alexander Leonard Truman, Kylie Nicole, Ryan Charles and Oliver Miles Truman.

"Passion without Justice" is his fifth published book.

The Editor

Professor Roy Wilson recently retired after teaching Journalism at Sheridan College Institute of Technology and Advanced Learning, in Oakville, Ontario since 1980. At various times he taught news and feature writing, law and ethics, municipal government, tabloid page design, supervised the weekly production of the Sheridan Sun newspaper and Sun on Line website and served as co-coordinator of the program and as a member of the Academic Council. He earned a Bachelor of Journalism degree at Carleton University, in Ottawa.

His industry experience in southern Ontario includes work in weekly and daily newspapers, magazines, television, radio and public relations. He has received newspaper and magazine awards at the provincial, national and international level. He has been treasurer of the Ontario Journalism Educators Association, and conducted page design seminars for the Ontario Community Newspapers Association across the province for many years.

ISBN 142514199-4